Twelve Ways of Mission
through Englesea Brook 1983-2011
and Mow Cop 1983-2019

Stephen Hatcher

British Library Cataloguing in Publication Data.
A catalogue record for this book is available from the British Library

ISBN 978 0 86071 887 1

A Commissioned Publication Printed by

MOORLEYS
Print, Design & Publishing
info@moorleys.co.uk · www.moorleys.co.uk

CONTENTS

By the same author:

Primitive Methodist Bibliography, Moorleys Print, Design and Publishing (2020) 228p

The Englesea Brook Story 1983-2011, Moorleys Print, Design and Publishing (2021) 208p

Education at Englesea Brook 1997-2011, with reference also to Education at Mow Cop,
Moorleys Print, Design and Publishing (2021) 53p

Introduction

The Christian Church generally aims to base its beliefs and activity on 'Scripture'. Over the years and especially over many generations Christian Churches also gather 'Traditions' - many of which can be helpful. Ultimately however the 'bar' to which all such 'Traditions' are brought is that of 'Scripture'. Thus what may be purely human additions may be helpful, but they must never be made essential for salvation.

Sometimes later developments *mirror* 'Scripture' closely. It has sometimes even been asserted that the beginning of the Primitive Methodist movement was 'just like' the *Acts of the Apostles* all over again - but in a different age, in a different location and with different leaders. Hugh Bourne the carpenter and William Clowes the potter were both 'working men' - so were the fishermen who became the first four disciples.

The character of the early Primitive Methodist movement was similar also. They met in the open air for their 'camp meetings' when they were members of the Methodist Connexion, and for this they were excluded from the Wesleyan Society. Jesus began his ministry teaching in the synagogue, but he also finished up in the open air when the authorities moved against him.

It is recognised that there is a broad parallel between the two spiritual movements - namely the *Acts of the Apostles* and the development of early Primitive Methodism. However this document seeks to explore further back into the unfolding of the Gospel story than that. The question is raised: Are there in fact a number of other 'parallels' that can be made between the *Gospel According to St Mark* as the earliest Gospel that we have in its present form, and the spiritual dynamic of the Primitive Methodist movement?

The document that follows identifies twelve themes of Christian Faith and Life that are contained within the Gospel according to St Mark. A parallel for each of these in then identified within Primitive Methodist tradition. It is believed that by looking at Scripture and Primitive Methodist belief and practice *together* will bring greater illumination when thinking today about mission in the contemporary world.

This document can be used by individuals and it can also be used as a group study course. Such a course will be successfully undertaken if the participants ask just three questions:

1) What did this passage mean to St Mark and the Early Christians? Why was it chosen for inclusion in the written Gospel?

2) Is our understanding of this passage 'illuminated' when set alongside Primitive Methodist faith and practice? And vice versa!

3) Looking at both Scripture (the passage in St Mark) and Tradition (Primitive Methodist engagement), what do we conclude for ourselves today?

NB. When a 'date' is quoted in brackets in the text then this is a reference taken from my diaries.

Preliminary

Englesea Brook Chapel had failed as a chapel for a number of reasons. Englesea Brook as a community was a hamlet with a very small population. Social habits had changed since the chapel had been built and most of the population now living in late 20thC society in Englesea Brook had never been 'chapel-going' folk. As a chapel it thus had little appeal.   The faithful older generation had got smaller and smaller and now the inevitable end had been reached.   If Englesea Brook Chapel was again to touch spiritual need, some really radical new thinking was required.

Would it fare any better as a museum?   Not necessarily, and as a Methodist museum it would probably fail even more dramatically than as a chapel.   What's the point of seeing a walking stick that once belonged to Hugh Bourne if you have no knowledge of who this man was and you also have very little interest in finding out!

So if Englesea Brook Chapel and Museum was to succeed in the future it must reach a new audience in significant numbers, generate significant income and become sustainable - how could it possibly do this?

Thus the Campaign to save the Englesea Brook Chapel which had begun in 1983 was viewed with a considerable degree of scepticism and even opposition from some quarters.   This was not surprising - to them it was just another failed rural chapel. To make matters worse it carried the burden of a graveyard with broken walls and overgrown graves. Where were the resources to be found? Where in the hamlet of Englesea Brook were the future members of the congregation now hiding?   In the critics' eyes it was nonsense.

What was surprising was that thirteen years later the 'enthusiasts' were still steaming ahead, and about to begin phase two on an even bigger scale. By 1996 a great deal of work had been done to the fabric, a display had been set up, a warden had been appointed and the premises were open on a Saturday and Sunday afternoon. Thus in the light of the progress made during the previous 13 years permission was granted by the Methodist Church for the development of Englesea Brook to continue, and on a vastly larger scale. A transition would be made in terms of my own time - from at most one day a week part-time activity from a distance of 100 miles away, up to locally based full-time activity from September 1996. It was a very big step up and I was keen to engage.

Unfortunately the purchase of 25 Queens Avenue, Tunstall (the proposed future domestic residence) was delayed and it looked as if the paperwork would take at least another month to complete.   The move out of the Grassington manse had to be made as another minister was waiting to take up occupancy and begin his work there from 1 September. So in fact when the new Methodist year began on 1 September 1996 I was living with my elder son at Mow Cop in the home of John and Ann Anderson. We were in receipt of their very kind hospitality. This meant that my son was able to start at his new school right from the beginning of the new academic year and this was a very great help to him.   I was also fully on the spot to begin my own work. My wife and younger children went to stay with relatives.

The task immediately ahead was to clear up after the 1996 book-sale at Mow Cop Chapel. In the past this had sometimes not been easy - who would want the 'leftovers' from a substantial sale with a large number of customers already having taken the pickings? On this occasion however the clearing-up was comparatively straight-forward. Jane Mansergh, a bookseller at Settle, a former museum curator, and a keen supporter of the 'vision' for Englesea Brook had kindly indicated that she was willing to take *all* that was left. The residue had largely come in cardboard boxes, there were still sufficient boxes to hand to re-box the surplus and one van was sufficient to carry it. (5/6 Sept 1996)

The next main task was to visit the Property Office at Manchester to report 'arrival' to the Rev. Kenneth Street and to outline 'plans'. The Property Office had most graciously supported the desire to do 'something constructive and something contemporary' at Englesea Brook; and to assist this goal had offered paid work in the form of a research project for the Property Division. This was sufficient to ensure that the total projected income for the Englesea Brook project would sustain activity during the first two years.

Thus a weekly visit to the Property Office was commenced to explore the records and identify chapels still in use throughout the country that were Primitive Methodist in origin. The aim was then to cross-reference this with data from historic Primitive Methodist publications.

The Property Office indicated that they often received requests from chapels asking a very basic question: Do you have anything that will help us with the history of our chapel? The request would then continue something like this: In two years' time we will celebrate the centenary of the present building but we have no records, can you help? So the question was put: would it be possible to match information from historic Primitive Methodist publications such as the *Magazine* and the *Christian Messenger* with 'live' contemporary chapels? If so this could mean that information about history and development could be supplied to local people via the Property Office when special commemorations / anniversaries came along.

This could also greatly enhance the occasion (and that chapel's publication) with real details about real people, rather than just having a date-stone - but little more.

In due course some of this research would also lead on to *Vision 2000* and the experience of chapels again becoming 'community hubs' because a kitchen and toilets had been added. Alternatively if the chapel already had these facilities then perhaps the requirement that was needed was a comfortable meeting room. There was no doubt about it - through this injection of 'practical hope' - in some cases the dying did come back to life as statistics of 'activities' and 'attendance' showed.

I will always be grateful for the financial support that this gave to Englesea Brook during these years of its 'second infancy', and also I am very grateful for having been privileged to work in this constructive role for the Methodist Property Office. (10, 17, 26 Sept, 22/24 Oct 1996 etc.)

A visit to the people of Englesea Brook was another high priority. Would there be speculation and anxiety in that small community about what might be proposed for the Chapel? Englesea Brook was the kind of sleepy hamlet where nothing ever happened, and many of the residents.

were quite at ease about it being like that...It was decided that there was no better way of nipping 'rumours in the bud' than by making the first move at an early stage. The local people were visited, questions were raised and answered, and friends were made (15 Sept 1996). At that early stage a number of strong friendships were also established and then sustained throughout the years.

During this first month of being 'on site' Bob Mealings, Curatorial Adviser for Cheshire Museums, was also contacted (19 Sept 1996). He, and his successor Tim Heathcote, couldn't often offer money - as the source from the County gradually dried up, however they always offered good advice and it was always well worth talking to them.

Prior arrangement had also already been made with a number of local circuit superintendents to preach during the late summer and autumn. These Sunday visits were as follows: Nantwich (6 Oct); Stoke South (13 Oct); Congleton (20 Oct); Leek (27 Oct); Hanley (3 Nov); Biddulph and Mow Cop (10 Nov); Northwich (17 Nov); Sandbach and Alsager (24 Nov); Newcastle (1 Dec); Burslem (8 Dec); Kidsgrove (15 Dec). All the many circuits within the Chester and Stoke-on-Trent Methodist District at that time would be offered Sunday preaching in due course and many friends were made.

On Sunday 22 September 1996 the Connexion and the District visibly demonstrated support for the project. The official 'launch' to the public was chaired by the Rev. Dr. Brian Powley the Chair of the Chester and Stoke-on-Trent District, and the Rev. Kenneth Street the General Secretary of the Property Division came to preach (22 Sept 1996).

This District support would continue, not only through the term of office of Brain Powley, but also through the term of office of his successor the Rev. John Walker. It had been rumoured in advance of his arrival that John Walker was a 'high churchman' and it was further wondered whether he would cope with Englesea Brook! It fact he was magnificent, John and his wife Janet gave themselves whole-heartedly to the cause and Janet also regularly attended the mid-week bible study group.

Indeed while making reference to District Chairmen as they were known back in the 1980s credit must also be given to the Rev. Stuart Rhodes. At that time (the early 1980s) the Chester and Stoke-on-Trent District through its various committees had given careful consideration to the case of Englesea Brook in response to the pleas of the superintendent of the Wolstanton and Audley Circuit the Rev. David Woolf. With regret it had been decided that nothing could be done other than to proceed to a sale.

However not all local people were satisfied with that decision - partly because they believed that there was a strong case for a future at 'Englesea Brook' and also partly because they believed that the Wolstanston Methodist Church had its eye on the sale proceeds for its own substantial building programme. My own misfortune was that now I had stirred a hornets' nest in the Chester and Stoke-on-Trent District by preparing an article for the *Methodist Recorder* - making a case for the retention and development of the chapel at Englesea Brook. This was not the kind of mine-field that Stuart Rhodes relished. However I was invited to his manse for a drink of coffee, a couple of scones and a conversation in which he was extremely gracious to me.

Within the District he was in a difficult position as he could not be a front-line 'cheer leader' in support.   However at the same time I left with no doubt that he wished me well.

Subsequently within the first four months up to the end of December 1996 a number of positive signals were also received from local people living at Englesea Brook that gave a message that was simply 'We are on your side'. For instance:

1) One of the neighbours asked for a discussion with the chapel leadership about how co-operation could take place to avoid conflict in traffic management in the region of the site. There was only limited roadside parking in front of the graveyard and to an extent on the grass verge going up the hill - and the demand for space far exceeded the supply of land.

2) Weston Parish Council through Cllr. M Turner offered a sack of daffodil bulbs for planting during the autumn on the bank and top of the front grass so that there would be a glorious bright yellow display in the spring.   This we did - and there was.

3) South and East Cheshire Technical College initiated a conversation about the possibility of a teacher placement at Englesea Brook.   They also advised that if we wished to visit a successful museum built on a 'religious theme' and with school groups visiting continually then we should 'sit in' at the Jewish Museum at Manchester where we would learn a lot - and we did on 10 December 1996. Visitors from the Jewish Museum a decade later then made a return visit to Englesea Brook to see what we had done (28 June 2007).

4) Janice Mary Sutch Pickard the Vice President of Conference visited Englesea Brook to hear about the 'plans', and a Weston couple Kenneth and Brenda West who were married in the chapel 50 years earlier returned to the Chapel to give thanks and to seek God's continuing blessing on their union (22 Dec 1996).

This was all very 'good going' for the first four months from a standing start.

Acknowledgements
I thank my wife Julia and my children for the constant support that they have offered. Without that support my own move to the geographical area where Englesea Brook is located would not have been possible.   The move to the 'Chester and Stoke-on-Trent District of the Methodist Church' changed the course of all of their lives and I express deep gratitude to them for their willing acceptance of this new direction.

I thank those who are named in the text, and many who are not so named, for the wonderful support I have received since my arrival in North Staffordshire.

I also thank those with whom I have discussed the text of this publication and those who have carefully 'proof read' what I have written: Janet Field, Margaret Gleave, Julia Hatcher, Randle Knight, David Scott and Margaret Veal. The final decisions made are of course my own.

1) Mission Through Engaging Minds (The Library)

Mark 1 vv.21-28 A New Teaching

Mark 1 v.22: The people who heard him were amazed at the way he taught, for he wasn't like the teachers of the Law; instead, he taught with authority.

What is this? Is it some kind of new teaching? (Mark 1 v.27) Mark raises a vital question at an early stage in his Gospel. Jesus had been baptised, he had called four fishermen and he had visited the local synagogue. At the synagogue he had 'cast out an evil spirit' from a distressed man who had also come to worship. The congregation who witnessed this event were truly amazed. Here was a new teaching and a new authority.

The impact made by the early ministry of Jesus cannot be over-stated, and this is an important point to grasp. The Gospel according to St. Matthew relates this theme to the *Sermon on the Mount* and thus also makes a wider point - the *whole* of the teaching of Jesus was with a new authority! (Matt 7 v.29)

Similarly the attempt to set up a 'Heritage Centre for Primitive Methodism' was a whole new idea and substantially at variance with current thinking within the Methodist Church at that time. In summary, contemporary thinking went something like this: Methodist Union took place in 1932; there are now no prefixes to the word 'Methodist'. We are now all Methodists - full stop. The official argument often continued: Of course due recognition of Wesley is appropriate. All the branches of Methodism go back to him and thus Epworth Old Rectory, the New Room Bristol, and Wesley's Chapel London all have a place in the one Methodist Church.

To gain attention for the Primitive Methodists it was necessary to argue that here from 1807 there was a subsequent phase of Christian endeavour and achievement. This story broke new ground and here also was an inspirational story to tell. Further, here was a story that was highly relevant.   It was also necessary to argue that if the story was to be told then 'resources' would help enormously! Thus significance was claimed for a comprehensive collection of Primitive Methodist printed literature, ephemera, circuit plans, ceramics and artefacts that had already been collected.

It was only because the argument was won that such a collection then moved from a private dwelling to be based at Englesea Brook Chapel. As the project developed 'the library' was further moved to Brookside Cottage which provided not only space for storage of books, but study and overnight accommodation for the researcher. Thus a local contemporary resource for a 'whole new area of teaching' was established, and a resource that was discovered to be pertinent to contemporary Methodist life. .

Historically there was a significant collection of printed Primitive Methodist literature that was part of Hartley Victoria College library. When that college closed that collection then became part of the Methodist Archives at the John Rylands University Library, Manchester. There was also a Wesley Historical Society Library (WHS) with some Primitive Methodist material at City Road, London adjacent to Wesley's Chapel, and this was moved at a later date to the library then situated at Oxford Brookes University.   However both the Rylands Library collection and that of the WHS were very far from being complete. The aim was that a library would be established at Englesea Brook Chapel and Museum that would have the role of dramatically extending the sphere of source material and study for many researchers. The aim was a bigger pool in which to fish, bigger fish to catch, and an enlarged knowledge of the subject matter in consequence. Of course this was a very big vision, and it has only been partly fulfilled.

In fact this personal quest to make a library of books about Primitive Methodism started back in the late 1960s before there was any thought of a major collection of artefacts on such a theme, and long before there was any thought of a Methodist Heritage Site at Englesea Brook. The concept of a 'centre' with staff, volunteers, a museum, lectures, a library, visiting public and educational programmes for schools was not in the late 1960s/early 1970s even a twinkle in the eye.

Having left Richmond College, London in 1968 my first circuit appointment was in the Holmfirth Circuit. This was sufficiently close to Manchester to be able to make a visit once a week when required for Probationer's Studies to Hartley Victoria Methodist College to use the library.

Contrary to my expectation, the significance of the Primitive Methodists, and the current neglect of this part of the history of Methodism *was* recognised in this West Yorkshire Methodist District. The District Chairman the Rev. Tom Morrow, although from a Wesleyan background himself nonetheless had a keen interest in Methodist history - post-Wesley, and he recognised the significance of the Primitive Methodist movement. The Rev. Martin Yeomans, the probationers' secretary was the son of a Primitive Methodist minister the Rev. Walter Yeomans who entered Hartley College in 1914. This may also have helped!   Contact was also made by Martin Yeomans with the Rev. Henry Rack at Hartley Victoria College to request some supervision. Thus a study of *Primitive Methodism* during the three years of probation was begun (1968-1971).

Initially this was conceived as a study; there was no thought of creating a library. However although Hartley library was very strong on bound volumes of Primitive Methodist periodicals it was very weak on biography, local history, theology and overseas missions - to name just a few of the categories where an enquirer might hope to find material. There was an urgent need to look elsewhere. Second-hand booksellers were consulted but this yielded little, so recourse was taken to the sending out of a letter to each of the 300 former Primitive Methodist ministers who were then largely retired - but who were still part of this world rather than the next. Thus the seven week postal strike during the early months of 1971 was used to prepare the 300 letters waiting for the day when post boxes would again be cleared. These ministers were simply asked: Can you help?   A considerable number responded with great generosity, the books came flooding in and a substantial library was born.

It was recognised that these were not books that many would view as fitting in well with the *Death of God* theology of the 1960s and early 1970s - which was highly praised by many younger theological minds. Generally within those minds these 'Prim' titles would be seen as of little value because they were judged to be just 'out of date' and in consequence no longer of any relevance in the world of *The Christian Agnostic*.

However it was believed that the reason for this negative interpretation was generally because such books were not viewed in the *context* of the age in which they were set. They were just seen as 'out of date' in the modern world - full stop. Those making the engagement wanted their theology on a plate; they were not prepared 'to dig' in regard to both text and context and they missed a fuller picture of what the Spirit was saying. It was believed that an understanding of where the Spirit had led in the *context* of the past would help later followers to see what that same Spirit was saying to 'would be followers' in the present age as well.

It was believed that there was far more of worth in Primitive Methodism than was recognised by those riding the 'band wagon' of contemporary theological fashion. Thus the 'drive' was stimulated to collect every Primitive Methodist title that ever was - if possible! To have value the overview must be as comprehensive as possible.

The vast majority of books came from retired Methodist ministers, who had treasured these volumes, but equally feared that no-one would want them after they had gone. Bookshops and booksellers would also be of some limited help. The Barbican Bookshop on Fossgate, York was visited with great regularity, and Laurie Gage Books at Leigh-on-Sea was also visited. This was done by visiting the Gage shop itself in an attempt to scoop up more of those missing titles ahead of other customers. Customers who waited for the catalogue would find that not all items were now for sale; it was also hard to be 'first' for those books that still were available - it all depended on the time at which the post arrived!

Some ex-Primitive Methodist Chapels were also visited to see if remnants of a former library might still be lurking on the premises in some remote vestry cupboard or other 'black hole'. Lay folk with a Primitive Methodist background were contacted as well - for instance Mrs Winifred Murray the widow of the late Professor A Victor Murray - and she was most supportive.

As the pile of books steadily grew it became clear that the achievements of some of the Primitive Methodists were quite remarkable. Study of Primitive Methodist 'ideas' using the library that came into existence would lead to new thoughts and new inspiration - and this would lead to new activity in that world of the 1970s.

It was recalled that even in the first volume of *The Chronicles of Narnia: The Magician's Nephew,* the adventures began in a room where 'Every bit of the walls was lined with shelves and every bit of the shelves was full of books'. How appropriate that was.

By 2002 in addition to the library that I had collected at home there was also a library which had been created in two bookcases at Englesea Brook Chapel and this was out-growing the space available. These books had been extracted from the many books that had come in for 'book-sales'. Of course there was some duplication with the vast collection of Primitive Methodist literature that I had collected at home. However it was recognised that Brookside Cottage could offer the opportunity for these two collections to be brought together and with space for the library to grow further. It also offered a separate room for study and somewhere for researchers to stay for the night at very reasonable cost.

To purchase Brookside Cottage cost £130,000 - a formidable sum, but with hard work and generous giving the target was reached and the purchase made. Of course when it was not required by library users the cottage was also let to those exploring the wider heritage of North Staffordshire and South Cheshire. This led to the making of many new friends and the significant generation of income. The land at the rear provided parking space for half a dozen vehicles when there was an event at the chapel, while two large sheds also at the rear

3

of Brookside accommodated equipment such as the funeral bier and tricycles for the school programmes that were also unfolding.

A vital part of this development was that it was a sound financial investment for the longer term: the income from the letting of the cottage was significantly more than the cost of running the cottage!   Thus financial support was provided from the cottage income for aspects of the project such as the running of the museum, which was labour-intensive and with much higher overheads.   The overall aim was of course to run the project as a whole 'in balance' and free from the need for 'grants' just as soon as possible.

The library was established downstairs in the front room of Brookside Cottage.   There was a locked fire door between that room and the rest of the cottage.   The *Pilgrim Trust* graciously paid for this upgrading of security and setting up of the library with a grant of £5000.   This grant would safeguard the library with secure locks on all external doors, and secondary glazing to stabilize the environment.   Also further additional security with window locks on all external windows was achieved - with enough of the grant remaining to provide shelving for the books.

A few years later the *Pilgrim Trust* provided a further grant of £10,000 to provide similar security and environmental well-being at Hough Chapel. This had been set up as a store for the increasing number of Primitive Methodist artefacts including banners which had been collected. Quite a lot of this collecting had been done on a 'van run' where the main purpose was to collect books for the various book-sales.   However banners and framed items could also be fitted safely into the van on top of the boxes of books, and then travel without damage and without additional transport costs to the Hough 'depot' of the Englesea Brook destination.

The library project was also most fortunate in the recruitment of qualified librarians to undertake the cataloguing. Alan Rose had acted as librarian initially but as time went on and demand increased it was recognised that it was essential to have someone local. Helen Prevett was the successful applicant for the post (1 Oct 2004, 13 Oct 2004, 22 Oct 2004, 20 Dec 2004) and at an early stage of her appointment she had the privilege of assisting Kevin Watson (a future director at Englesea Brook), who visited the Library from the University of Sheffield in connection with the preparation of his PhD (14 Oct 2004).

Later David and Rosemary Tonks took over as joint librarians and gave excellent service with the cataloguing and arrangement of books on the shelves, often working more than the one day a week to which they had made commitment as volunteers.   (24 Sept 2006, 14 Oct 2006).

They were also skilled in the recognition of a Primitive Methodist publication from the *place* of publication when that might not have been obvious from the subject matter. For instance take the following example:

ANTLIFF, William, *The Life and Labours of the Late Thomas Morgan,* London, King (1856) 152p. Is this a Primitive Methodist book? How do you know? The answer is that William Antliff was a significant Primitive Methodist author and because his name is known it is also known that this is a book that should be in the library. Thomas Morgan was also a Primitive Methodist itinerant and his name can be found on William Leary's published list of such. In fact it is an extremely rare book and a copy has never been found for the Englesea Brook library - so keep your eyes open.

That was an easy one to recognise! However there are many books where the identification is much more difficult. What about the following one?

BARNES, James, *The Devil Himself and how to Conquer Him,* London, Ralph Fenwick (1884) 93 + iii p   The biggest clue on the title page here is the name of the Primitive Methodist book steward who published the volume - Ralph Fenwick.   However if this was not known this title might have been missed and sent down to the Hassall Road Book Room to be sold! Thus the volunteer librarians did an outstanding job in setting up the library. They knew what they were doing and if they didn't they were not afraid to ask.

In making key texts of Primitive Methodist literature more readily available Phil Roberts rendered excellent service also through 'Tentmaker Publications'.   Three early and very scarce Primitive Methodist publications were reprinted by 'Tentmaker', supplied in hard cover and made available for sale at a very reasonable price (19 Sept 2004).

They were:
Walford, John, *The Life and Labours of the Venerable Hugh Bourne*, 2 vols
Clowes, William, *Journals*, or the *Life of William Clowes*
Herod, George*, Biographical Sketches of some of those Preachers whose labours contributed to the Origination and Early Expansion of the Early Primitive Methodist Connexion*

Later the two volumes by H B Kendall, *The Origin and History of the Primitive Methodist Church* were also re-printed (26 Oct 2006).

With these books again in print no-one needed to be without basic source material to get them started on their research project.   The re-prints would whet the appetite, and this would often then be followed up by researchers wanting to make a visit to Brookside Cottage to consult manuscripts, circuit plans, books and other printed ephemera.

(NB. At the time of writing Bookside Cottage is no longer Methodist property, the researcher should contact the Museum Director for information about the current arrangements for access to literature.)

Question: Where do we find our 'authority' today? Do we find it in the Bible, in the teaching of the Church, or within our own experience?

Girl in costume, reading

A visit to Englesea Brook Chapel and Museum was always a 'learning experience'. It could be as a visit to the Victorian Working-Class Sunday School for a 'day out' with other class-mates from a local primary school. In this case a simple reading book that began with the letters of the alphabet would be used.

It could be study that was spread over several months or even years as part of the research for a PhD. Alternatively by staying for a week in the cottage and with concentrated research it was possible for a new article to be produced by those already well-established in the academic world. Professor David Bebbington and Professor Robert Colls each stayed for a week on different occasions with this objective in mind.

Professor Robert Colls teaching at Mow Cop

It has been a great pleasure to listen to Prof. Robert Colls at Englesea Brook and Mow Cop on a number of occasions over the years. He is the author of number of titles that relate to the society, life, work and faith of colliers in the north-east of England. Among his published works are:

The Collier's Rant, Song and Culture in the Industrial Village, London, Croom Helm (1977) 216p

'The Forgotten World of Christian Socialism' in: *History Today*, March 2015 pp.37-39

The Pitmen of the Northern Coalfield, Work, Culture, Protest 1790-1850, Manchester University Press (1987) 386p

'Primitive Methodists in the Northern Coalfields' pp.323-334 in: OBELKEVICH, Jim, ROPER, Lyndal, SAMUEL, Raphael, *Disciplines of Faith: Studies in Religion, Politics and Patriarchy* (1987) 581p

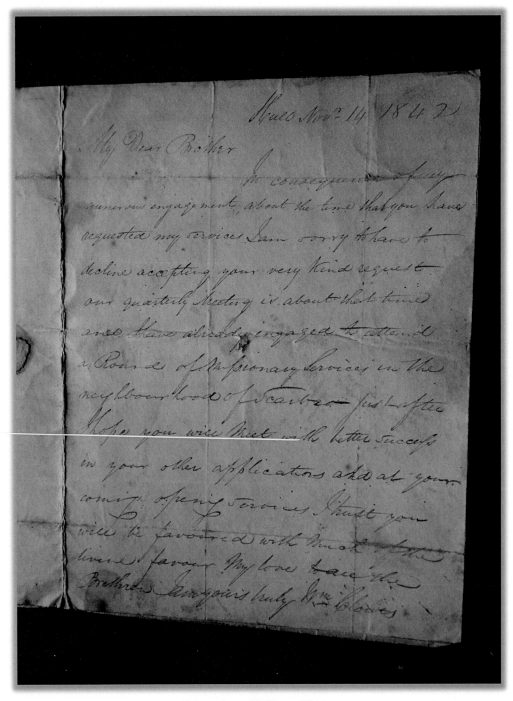

Letter from William Clowes

This letter was written by Clowes and sent from Hull to Mansfield and dated Nov 14 1842. It has been stamped by the postal services at both 'Hull' and 'Mansfield'.

It reads:

My Dear Brother, In consequence of my numerous engagements about the time that you have requested my services I am sorry to have to decline accepting your very kind request, and our quarterly meeting is about that time. Also I have already engaged to attend a round of missionary services in this neighbourhood of Scarbro' just after.

I hope that you will meet with better success in your applications and at (?) your coming opening services. I trust that you will be favoured with much divine favour.
With love to all the Brethren, I am yours truly Wm. Clowes.

2) Mission Through an On-site Experience: 'Within These Walls'
(The Buildings: Mission Through the Chapel and Museum from Within)

Mark 2 vv.1-12 Jesus Heals a Paralysed Man

Mark 2 v.4: So they made a hole in the roof right above the place where Jesus was.

Jesus was in a domestic dwelling, and the crowd that had flocked towards him had filled the place inside and had also jammed the entrance.   Within those walls he was far less accessible. (We trust that when Jesus is 'within the walls of a church' today - this makes Him *more* accessible to the world outside rather than less.).   However in the biblical story those who needed him most were driven to the extremity of making for the roof, creating a hole and lowering a man on a mattress down to where Jesus was speaking below.

Primitive Methodists may be best remembered for their open air 'camp meetings' which of course were 'without walls' and freely open to all.   However it is important to recognise that at Harriseahead Hugh Bourne first took a leading role at a cottage meeting held at Old Jane Hall's house some six years before the 1807 camp meeting at Mow Cop.

As H B Kendall reports:
Soon after the revival began, a weekly cottage prayer meeting was established at Jane Hall's - for long the only Methodist at Harriseahead. At the first meeting held here, Hugh Bourne 'broke through splendidly'. He had attempted to pray at Ridgway the previous Sunday, but the result was not encouraging. From this time, he notes, 'he was fitted to be a public praying labourer'.   The prayer meetings thus instituted were not of the ordinary kind. Here again everybody was expected to take part, and *liveliness* was the characteristic.   'The people got to be, in great measure, Israelitish', says Hugh Bourne, which we find, being interpreted, means - very noisy. Bourne quoted Ezra 3 v. 13 'And all the people shouted with a great shout….and the noise was heard afar off.' This was strictly true of the 'Israelitish' prayer meetings held at Jane Hall's. Hugh Bourne tells how it happened. The door of a house on Mow Cop was standing open and Elizabeth Baddeley, a miner's wife, who was given to the use of profane language, distinctly heard the sound of prayer and praise coming from Harriseahead a mile and a half away. She was convinced of sin, and set out for heaven.

As the Primitive Methodist movement developed it appears that the camp meeting became an annual event.   So where did they meet the rest of the time?   It is clear that a vast amount of the 'winning' and the 'building up' of converts to the faith was done 'within walls'.   This could be within a cottage kitchen, a barn, or as at Tunstall in a new building in the shape of 'four cottages' so that, in that instance, an alternative use could be found when the time came to move on.   The success at Tunstall was such that 'the move on' was a 'move up'- a move to a bigger chapel, and this success was repeated in many other places.

Within the walls of the Englesea Brook Chapel a considerable number of ways of engaging with visitors have been chosen over the years.   First of all the chapel is an artefact itself and tells a story about worship in a pre-Victorian and Victorian world - with pulpit, pews and box pews upstairs. There is also a harmonium, a clock, and a grave stone in the aisle.   These are all long-standing aspects of the chapel interior.

Secondly, there is now what in earlier years was used as the former schoolroom. This has now become far more obviously a museum. Various displays in glass cases, display boards and a working museum exhibit have been set up. This 'working exhibit' was once the printing press that was used by the Bourne brothers at Bemersley.

These buildings which constitute the Englesea Brook site are comparatively small so the aim from the beginning was to 'pack in as much as possible'. In sound and vision, through the static and in motion, through the observed and the experienced, the chapel and its collection communicate with the visitor.

Here are a few examples of the imaginative ways in which the building and its contents have communicated to the visitor in the years from the 1990s. For instance the sound of the playing of the small pipe organ which was brought from Silsden was triggered by a sensor in the chapel when visitors opened the door and stepped inside. They were thus greeted by an authentic Primitive Methodist tune such as 'Hark the Gospel News is Sounding', and with the notes actually played on the early 'Primitive' organ that they could see at the back of the chapel and dating from pre-Victorian times. At least this stimulated a sense of surprise in a visitor who was now thinking 'that was interesting, I wonder what will happen next?' At best it helped to create an authentic atmosphere for the visit that was about to take place.

There were also handsets in the chapel with recorded oral history, and when lifted the voice of Janet Field providing the context for the narration could be distinctly heard. Ken Howarth of the North West Sound Archive was asked to lead this project which included a day's training for those who were to conduct the interviews and make the recordings. Handsets were provided for the chapel and the oral history recording started to play the moment the handset was lifted. The cost of the recording of the playing of the organ was included in this package making a total figure of £4,962 for this equipment including the various recordings that it contained. The visitor experience was considerably enhanced and would be for many years to come (21 February 1998).

On arrival in the museum section of the site the visitor also discovered that there was verbal and visual engagement which included an audio-visual introduction to the collection. The doors were opened on the front of the model of Filey Ebenezer Chapel and this revealed a screen behind and inside the model. (The model itself was a very good representation - having been made in the Cheshire Museums workshop).

The visitors were asked if they would like to view the eight minute audio-visual introduction. The green button was pressed and as the picture flickered for a moment on the screen the visitors were also asked if they would like a complimentary cup of tea or coffee to drink while they watched the video. The kettle had already boiled so within a couple of minutes it was possible to supply the tea and coffee along with a chocolate digestive biscuit for each visitor.

One highlight of the tour was the seven 'virtual reality' flames in the museum with the themes taken from *The Seven Lamps of Architecture* by John Ruskin. These 'flames' and the associated display explored the words used by Ruskin with a biblical and Primitive Methodist application. The words that Ruskin chose were: Beauty, Life, Truth, Memory, Obedience, Sacrifice and Power. For more about these flames see chapter 6. The pulpit contained the largest flame which underlined the power of the preaching of the word. At an earlier stage before the 'flames' were introduced the pulpit contained a life-sized model made in papier-mache of a female preacher. This effectively made a point about the significance of early female preachers within Primitive Methodism. She was given pride of place!

The atmosphere created by the rousing *Primitive* music and the seven 'burning and shining lights' (to use a Primitive Methodist 'catch-phrase') in a darkened room, was quite remarkable.

Before the small extension was built at the rear of the premises bars were put over the small external window for security. With the building of the extension which included a new back door the barred window was no longer in an external wall. There were three options: it could be left as it was, or the bars could be taken off as they were no longer needed, or it could be turned into a 'feature'. The third route was chosen - the bars became the bars of a prison and at the push of a button the prisoner (Thomas Russell) would tell the viewer why he was there.

In the same room created by the building of the extension the magic lantern was set up. Pews were placed against the two side walls, the projector (a real magic lantern running on 12 volts of electricity supplied from a step-down transformer on the wall) gave the light, and the image of the magic lantern glass slide appeared on a screen in front of the window of the former school-room. As the magic lantern light was just 12 volts had any significant external light intruded the image on the screen would have been of very poor quality indeed. However the one external light source in that room was supplied through the roof light and with the help of a long pole and sliding partition - this was 'blacked out' in an instant. With a quick movement of the arm a panel was slid from one side of the roof-window to the other in a flash, and this achieved near total black-out. In this way it was possible to give to those crowded into the small room below the authentic magic lantern experience.

Magic lantern slides which were the gift of the Rev Dr John T Wilkinson were used most often. These contained some of the images that can also be found in H B Kendall's two volume work to mark the bi-centenary: *The Origin and History of the Primitive Methodist Church.* These images were colour-tinted and thus using authentic magic lantern slides on an authentic magic lantern heightened the value of this part of the tour - as long as the operator could also narrate the story at the same time as manipulating the slides. Fortunately the commentary was known by heart and written text was definitely not needed!

Occasionally a special additional attraction would be added at the museum. For instance on the 20 April 2000, £400 was paid for £900 worth of flowers that were purchased from M J Steel at Little Island Nursery (A discount for bulk buying and a 'good cause'). The flower festival was open for just five days, visited by approximately 1000 visitors with takings of £1,587 13p. That was 1000 people who visited the premises, many for the first time - and many of those would come back!

The picture painted in Mark 2 is of the building so crowded that entry from the roof for the paralytic was judged to be the only way in. Such a point of extremity was never reached at Englesea Brook, rather over the years there has been a vast succession of visiting groups coming in an orderly manner. However on the 2 November 2000 a communication was received from Weston and Basford Parish Council expressing concern about the number of vehicles parked in Englesea Brook of those visiting the museum. This of course underlined what was already known at that time - namely the urgent need for off- street parking. This stimulated further discussions about the ownership of the chapel drive.

Could the chapel 'buy out' the other party with whom joint use was shared, and could the chapel establish exclusive use?   If so this could provide at least some limited additional parking as well as easier access.   At the other side of the Chapel Cottages on what had formerly been chapel property there was sufficient land for 6 to 8 cars to park, but this land had been sold for 'next to nothing' along with the two cottages by the Wolstanton and Audley Circuit, before the Englesea Brook Management Group were able to take control - and there was no chance of buying that land back...   Oh how hard the Methodist Church sometimes makes life for itself!

To underline the point the following is a small sample of a few of the great variety of different groups visiting Englesea Brook during the next few years and illustrating the reality of the need for parking space, as well as the great opportunity.   They were also far from all being 'dyed in the wool, card carrying, paid up members' of the Methodist Church:

53 seater coach party from Llanymynech Circuit am; 53 seater coach party from Stafford Circuit pm (18 July 1998).   That was two coach parties in one day!

Coventry and District Archaeological Society in 2 mini-buses (5 April 1999)

National Trust, North Staffs Group (18 May 2000)

College of the Third Age (14 Sept 2000)

Terry Dunn Walking Group – but they all of course arrived in cars (3 Jan 2002)

Audlem History Society

Busy Bees Holiday Scheme - a group of 30 children and leaders from New Moston, Manchester (2 June 2004)

Rainhill, Prescott Group am (14 visitors), and Darlington Street Men's Group pm (36 visitors) who also visited Mow Cop. (12 June 2004)

Woore W I Group (10 Aug 2005)

Coach party from Wigan visiting Bridgemere 11.00am, Englesea Brook 2.30pm and Mow Cop for tea 4.30pm (1 June 2006)

Cameo Club (6 June 2006)

Ancient Order of Foresters (7 June 2006)

Abergele Field Club and Historical Society (10 June 2006)

William Porter and the Beacon Group (22 June 2006)

Marple Men's Group (27 June 2006)

Quinton Local History Society (15 July 2006)

Methodist Luncheon Club, Manchester (16 July 2006)

WEA Students (22 Aug 2006)

Liverpool District Men's Methodist Luncheon Club (25 April 2007)

Fortunately those who worked in the 'office' on the administration - Sue Frost, Delia Garratt, Keith Nixon and Margaret Veal, were also all very good at welcoming visitors, and they all knew instinctively when it was time to 'switch roles'.

Question: Where does the church best sustain its Life and conduct its Mission? Is this in a domestic dwelling or in a purpose built Church building - or where?

In the pews at Englesea Brook

In the Gospel story (Mark 2 vv.1-12) when part of a roof was removed a hole must have been created that was six feet long by at least two or three feet wide. For reasons of basic safety the patient must surely have descended on a stretcher that was kept in the horizontal plane while the lowering took place. Otherwise there would have been the risk of much further injury when the body reached the ground! The aim was not to add 'broken bones' to the existing paralysis. One can imagine the confusion of many within that room and perhaps the deep indignation of the home-owner who must have felt that his property was being wrecked. *Mission* doesn't always take place in a tidy fashion as is also demonstrated by those in the chapel excitedly opening storage boxes and trying on costume! However for them equally it was a real experience and entry into another world.

With a net at Mow Cop

Members of the Mow Cop congregation are holding a fisherman's net that was once used in Filey - by the fishermen there.   Initially in the early 1820s when Primitive Methodism was spreading throughout Yorkshire from its Hull base the Primitive Methodist missionaries found the clannish Filey fishermen extremely resistant to the Gospel message.   Johnny Oxtoby pleaded with his fellow preachers to give Filey one more chance. He went, he prayed, he preached and he conquered - in 1823 a remarkable revival took place among the Filey fishermen.   A small chapel was soon built and this was followed in 1870 by a grand edifice. Sadly in the later 20th Century when the fishing industry went into decline so did the number of fishermen and in due course the chapel closed.   However it was still affectionately remembered at Englesea Brook where the audio-visual introduction was housed within a model of that same Filey Ebenezer Chapel.

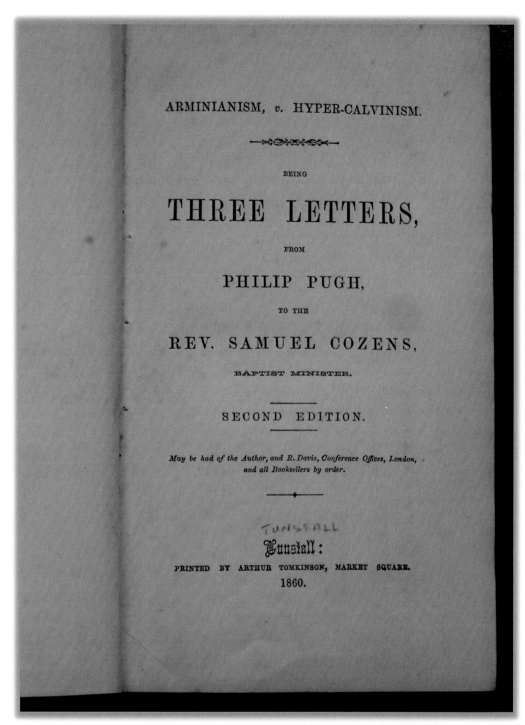

Doctrinally, PMs were Arminian not Calvanist -
Doctrinally, there were no walls

Philip Pugh was a significant Primitive Methodist Itinerant. While he was stationed in the prestigious Tunstall appointment where the Jubilee Chapel was opened in 1860 he prepared this major document to overthrow the erroneous teaching (as he saw it) of the Rev. Samuel Cozens a contemporary Baptist Minister. Sound teaching was essential:

'Man is a physical, intellectual, moral, and religious being, and the whole of his humanity must be subjected to healthy training'

'Tis education forms the common mind just as the twig is bent the tree's inclined'

(Pritchard, *Life and Labours Philip Pugh* p.274)

3) Mission to the Wider World: Sowing Seeds and Feeding Minds
(Education Near and Far)

Mark 4 vv.1-9 Jesus Teaches Through Parables

Mark 4 v.8: But some of the seeds fell in good soil, and the plants sprouted and grew, and produced corn.

Once there was a man who went out to sow corn
Jesus paints a picture of the many setbacks that the farmer will face. Some of the seed fell on the path and the birds came and took it away, some of it fell on rocky ground where there was little soil and some fell among thorn bushes. Yet despite these setbacks, even though some seed would be lost, nonetheless the harvest would come. It would be the same with the Kingdom of God.

Jesus saw an illustration of what he believed the Kingdom of God was like through his observation of a daily scene in his native Palestine. Yes a lot of the seed will be lost, but nonetheless the Kingdom of God will come.

Education, when offered by Englesea Brook was *seed* cast to the 'many' not the 'few'. During the early peak of Englesea Brook's work with schools, done with the assistance of David Scott and Margaret Gleave, over fifty schools were visited each term. In a majority of cases these visits were to take a whole school assembly. Some schools were small and rural but this was a minority, the vast majority were schools within the Stoke-on-Trent / Newcastle-under-Lyme conurbation. Here the number of children present for a 'whole school assembly' was likely to be at least two hundred and it could be twice that figure. If the average figure of those present in an assembly is taken as just two hundred pupils and staff this means that those fifty visits would reach ten thousand children in a term.

For instance, in 2010 during the twelve week period from Wednesday 6 January to Monday 29 March, engagement took place with thirty three schools by just one of the visitors. Usually this was to take an assembly, however very often these visits were also with 'class room time' after the assembly for the handling of artefacts and with the opportunity to ask questions. Here is an example of the ground covered by one of the school visitors both in relation to number of pupils involved and the geographical spread of the schools during that spring term of 2010:

Wednesday 6 January Forsbrook 200 pupils: The 1940s - Where was God?
Thursday 7 January Seabridge 300 pupils: Bus Conductors - Environmental care
Monday 11 January Castle, Mow Cop 80 pupils: The Penny Farthing - Will the preacher arrive?
Tuesday 12 January Hassall 240 pupils: The 1940s - Where was God?
Friday 15 January Alsager Highfields 200 pupils: The 1940s - Where was God?
Monday 18 January Woodcocks Well, Mow Cop 80 pupils: The Penny Farthing - Will the preacher arrive?
Tuesday 19 January 9.00am Weston Coyney 180 pupils: Bus Conductors - Environmental care
Tuesday 19 January 2.45pm Richard Heathcote: The 1940s - Where was God?
Wednesday 20 January Summerbank 180 pupils: Bus Conductors - Environmental care

Monday 25 January Bursley 180 pupils: The 1940s - Where was God?
Tuesday 26 January Langdale 180 pupils: Trains to Mow Cop
Thursday 28 January Bradwell 150 pupils: Through the Eyes of a Roman Soldier
Friday 29 January Eaton Park 450 pupils: Through the Eyes of a Roman Soldier
Monday 1 February St Chads, Red Street: Through the Eyes of a Roman Soldier
Tuesday 2 February Heron Cross 180 pupils: Through the Eyes of a Roman Soldier
Wednesday 3 February Weston Coyney 180 pupils: Through the Eyes of a Roman Soldier
Friday 5 February Spring Head, Talke Pits: Through the Eyes of a Roman Soldier
Monday 8 February Norton 150 + 45 pupils: Through the Eyes of a Roman Soldier
Monday 8 February Hillside, Baddeley Green 180 + 30 pupils: Trains to Mow Cop
Tuesday 9 February Sutherland 420 + 60 pupils: Through the Eyes of a Roman Soldier
Wednesday 10 February Goldenhill 160 + 30 pupils: Through the Eyes of a Roman Soldier
Thursday 11 February Mill Hill 400 + 60 pupils: Through the Eyes of a Roman Soldier
Friday 12 February Thursfield, Harriseahead 220 + 35 pupils: Through the Eyes of a Roman Soldier
Monday 22 February Excalibur, Alsager 195 + 28 pupils + 14 staff: Trains to Mow Cop
Tuesday 23 February St Paul's Edensor 130 pupils + 6 staff: Trains to Mow Cop
Wednesday 24 February Knypersley First 180 pupils + 6 staff: Through the Eyes of a Roman Soldier
1 March Woodcocks Well 85 pupils + staff: Through the Eyes of a Roman Soldier
3 March Thursfield, Harriseahead years 1 and 2: Bus Conductors - Environmental care
8 March St Chads at Englesea Brook, year 1 56 pupils: Through the Eyes of a Roman Soldier
11 March Goldenhill: Victorians at Englesea Brook
17 March Wybunbury Delves; year 2 Easter – Through the Eyes of a Roman Soldier
23 March Newstead 205 + 30: Easter – Through the Eyes of a Roman Soldier
29 March Weston Coyney Juniors year 3 x 2: Easter – Through the Eyes of a Roman Soldier

Education in the form of the 'Working-class Sunday School' experience was popular with older groups as well as with children. For instance the Cumbia Wesley Historical Society sent a coach with 47 visitors in total - most were adults but the group included 9 children. The whole party experienced the role play of the 'Working-class Sunday School' (18 May 2002).

Groups of children also visited from a distance for the Victorian Working Class Sunday School. For instance the 'Busy Bees Holiday Scheme from New Moston, Manchester brought 35 children for a 'day out' to Englesea Brook with Mrs Margaret Gleave as the teacher (27 April 2002, 8 August 2002).

At times older groups of students appeared. For instance John Bishop who taught Sociology to 'A' level students in the Humanities Department, at Wirral Metropolitan College made a visit with 9 students.

Sometimes the out-of-season months didn't bring many adult visitors to Englesea Brook. November for instance was often a poor month for adults but nonetheless a very good month for school visits. In the month of November alone in 2004 the record for school/educational visits to Englesea Brook was as follows:

Wednesday 3 Nov, Eaton Park Primary School year 6 (Margaret Gleave)
Thurday 4 Nov, Forsbrook Primary School year 6 (Margaret Done)

Friday 5 Nov, Eaton Park Primary School year 6 second class (Margaret Gleave)
Tuesday 9 Nov, Langdale Junior School year 5 (Margaret Gleave)
Wednesday 10 Nov, Langdale Junior School year 5 second class (Margaret Done)
Thursday 11 Nov, Mill Hill Primary School year 5 (Margaret Done)
Friday 12 Nov, Mill Hill Primary School year 5 second class (Margaret Gleave)
Monday 15 Nov, Bursley Primary School 55 pupils years 1 and 2 (Ann Beckett)
Wednesday 17 Nov, Bursley Primary School second group
Thursday18 Nov, Hillside Primary School, Baddeley Green
Tuesday 23 Nov, Queens Primary School, Fenton year 5 (Ann Beckett)
Wednesday 24 Nov, Wirral Metropolitan College 'A' level Sociology students
Wednesday 24 Nov, Rudheath Com.Primary School (1st group) 45 pupils (Margaret Gleave)
Thursday 25 Nov, Moor First School, Biddulph Moor Years 2/3/4, 49 pupils (Margaret Done)
Monday 29 Nov, Crescent Primary School Year 2 - 2 classes', 49 pupils (Ann Beckett)
Tuesday 30 Nov, Rudheath Com. Primary (2nd group) Year 6, 50 pupils (Margaret Done)

That makes approximately 570 school visitors to Englesea Brook for an educational visit during the one month of November. Three 'teachers' shared these dates between them: Ann Beckett, Margaret Done, Margaret Gleave.

The visits to schools whether for an 'assembly', classroom time or both, had indeed stimulated this significant response. The assembly visits had included the following:

Hugh Bourne: The story of his life was illustrated with three objects: A ruler reflected his life as someone 'working' as a carpenter. He was also the editor of the *Primitive Methodist Magazine.* His ruler was thus also used for drawing lines in pencil on his writing paper. He wrote letters and he kept a Journal.

A walking stick was used to describe his travels and the fact that he could walk up to forty miles a day. It was also boasted that he could achieve that on minimal sustenance - two hard boiled eggs and some dried bread.

A boot demonstrated that he stood firm and that he put his foot down on the camp meeting controversy. Bourne the moor-lander who spent his early years in isolation at Ford Hays Farm and his adult years at Bemersley was shy but tough. He was also confident that this was the work of God.

For ease of memory retention for the children it was noted that Hugh Bourne made his mark by 'working, walking and winning'.

William Clowes: The story of his life was illustrated with a Love Feast cup and walking stick. The Love Feast in early Methodism was a rediscovery of the early Christian Agape or fellowship meal. It also had similarities with the Sacrament of the Lord's Supper and William Clowes himself mistook it for such. He participated in a Love Feast having gained admission on someone else's ticket and was filled with dread least he had eaten and drunk unworthily. It was thus a turning point in his life and he went on to travel as a preacher of the Gospel. Clowes *Journals* report his missions to the north of England, London and Cornwall.

Thomas Russell: The story of his life, travels, imprisonment and hard labour was illustrated with his carpet bag. The story of Russell working at the wheel was vividly narrated.

The diet was atrocious, the labour was severe and the management was ruthless. 'He came here to be punished and punished he must be' was the response of those in Authority.

Johnny Oxtoby: The story of how in 1823 he prayed on Muston Hill for the fishermen who had rejected every previous attempt to win them for the Christian Gospel was told. However it was different this time. Thus he went with renewed confidence to preach and he won the Filey fishermen who turned from superstition to God. The story was illustrated with a fishing-net and a fisherman's gansey, both of which were from Filey and from the home of a direct descendant of those early fishermen.

The Filey Fishermen: The story was told of how their boat was blown out of the water and they were taken to meet the commander of the German U Boat submarine. However this was a story with a double 'happy ending'. First of all after interrogation the commander of the submarine offered the fisherman a small boat that the submarine was carrying so that they could row to land and they arrived in due course on the Northumberland coastline. The Filey community at this stage believed that the fishermen were 'lost' as three days had now past since they put to sea. However just imagine the rejoicing in Filey when the news reached that community that the fishermen were safe! It was also noted that those who were believed to be dead were discovered to be very much alive on the third day.

The Roman Soldier in costume was used to tell the Easter Story, the Christmas story, or to relate a memorable 'Parable' told by Jesus. Stationed in the Holy Land he had been an eye witness to some of the key events. At Christmas he was doing census duty and keeping order at Bethlehem. At Easter he was in Jerusalem and witnessed the crucifixion. (It could be objected: But these stories are not specifically Primitive Methodist, this is the basic Gospel message! It could be answered: Yes that is true, however these were the core beliefs of the Primitive Methodists - as of all Christian believers.)

The Bus Conductor in costume and with equipment (cap, jacket, badge, ticket rack, ticket punch, ticket bag with pre-decimal coinage) to promote public transport was used to illustrate community benefit and environmental care. The bicycle riding, bus travelling, pre-Beeching world of the 1940s was contrasted with the car-dominated, carbon dioxide emitting, 'global warming' world of today. (Again this is not specifically 'Primitive Methodist'; however it should be noted that these poor 'Prims' left only the lightest of carbon footprints behind them. Their lifestyle can be used to point to enlightened living within society today.)

Many of the Primitive Methodist preachers prior to 1932 walked to their Sunday preaching appointments. In rural areas this could mean a walk of several miles there and of course several miles home again afterwards as well. So after six days of working long hours in the fields Sunday was not a 'day of rest' for these preachers. However they saw their calling as preachers to be a way by which the central purpose of their lives could be fulfilled.

If the preacher travelled by bus to take his appointments then he might have a different issue of conscience. The bus crew were working on a Sunday for his benefit - was that right? Didn't they deserve a 'day of rest'? It was recognised that ethical issues change with the passage of time. What was a key issue then may not be so today! Thus questions were asked: What are the key issues today? Where is society most blind?

The Hornby Clockwork Train layout had a model of Mow Cop on a raised area at the centre of the 8 feet square train board. In the real world the visitor's journey would include a walk to the local station perhaps in a distant part of the country. Visitors would then take a ride on the train to Mow Cop and Scholar Green station and finally take a walk up the hill for the 1907 camp meeting.

The programmes that have been listed above were all mainly for children. However, there was also a remarkable amount of interest in these themes from adults also. The aim was always to enlarge the number of *ways* into the theme of 'Primitive Methodism' and hence to enhance the 'interest' of the museum for future visitors of all ages.

At the Museum itself additional 'features' were developed. The key issue, fundamental to the success of the whole project was faced. It was this: Englesea Brook as a place is a remote location and the chapel and museum constitute a small site. How is this to be made attractive to visitors? In terms of quality and quantity how can the site be developed so that it is of relevance, of interest and worth a visit? Further 'Primitive Methodism' itself sounds very 'minority' to put it politely, and quite likely to be 'boring', 'obscure' and 'irrelevant' to the world of today. However it was believed that there *was* and *is* an answer and what follows is a further part of that answer.

For instance in 1998 an **Oral History Training Programme** was put in place with recording of the memories of specially selected elderly visitors. The handsets to which reference has already been made were installed in the museum and this meant that the memories recorded were available for future visitors - simply at the lifting of the handset. One handset was located in the pulpit and another in the choir stall immediately in front of the harmonium. Modern technology and equipment sounded a note that led to many hours of happy listening.

As previously noted tunes played on the restored pipe organ were also recorded and this disc was triggered by a sensor. Thus when a newly-arrived visitor opened the door to the chapel the sound of the welcoming notes of the 1828 organ playing the Ranter tunes was clearly heard. This simple arrangement immediately raised the interest level of visitors. 'What else?' they wondered. A sense of expectancy was generated at the point of arrival The sound of the organ brought life and vitality to the premises, while the handsets offered authentic memories from those in a position to tell the story - because they had actually lived it.

Further on-site there was also a feature of a **Prisoner behind Bars.** By pressing a button the visitors could listen to a recording from Thomas Russell who suffered imprisonment with hard labour for selling religious literature to a police constable who had been 'set-up' to catch him out. It was alleged by the magistrate that he needed a hawker's licence, so from behind bars in what was known then as the 'extension' Thomas Russell was able to tell visitors why he was there - including the suffering that he experienced 'working at the wheel'. He told it well and visitors felt some of the pain.

Because of the key role of the work with schools and the growing success of this role it was decided to make the appointment of an Education Officer. This would be for a person with experience within secular education and who would bring to the post a committed Christian faith along with imagination and creativity. From a small pool of able applicants Mrs Margaret Veal was appointed and she went on to develop the role with imagination and major success. With the continuing success of the project a paid administrative role was also needed and Margaret Veal was also appointed to this until after my retirement. This paid work was quite apart from driving vans, shifting boxes of books along with the men and offering her garage as a local deposit for storage.   She is greatly to be thanked for her years of very faithful service.

Step by step Englesea Brook was engaging with the world.   The project was no longer seen just as a museum with boring objects in glass cases.   It was a heritage site of course and there were objects in glass cases, meticulous records were kept by Randle Knight *but* it was a heritage site which was fully engaged with the contemporary world and with a relevant voice.

As evidence of the growing interest of the wider world the following should be noted:

A study day was held jointly with the Keele University, on the Keele site and at the chaplain's invitation.   The theme was: 'A Re-discovery of New Testament Christianity?' - An Examination of Primitive Methodist Worship, Mission and Theology. A new audience was reached. (14 November 1998)

The year 1998 also ended with a recording made on the Englesea Brook premises that would reach the biggest audience as yet by far: The BBC came to record for a *Songs of Praise* programme. This was broadcast on Palm Sunday of the year ahead - 1999.

Off-site many churches and secular organisations were also becoming increasingly interested. For instance a study day was offered by the Potteries Theological Society where the title was: *Radical Christianity 1807-2007 Primitive Methodist insights for today* (26 April 2005).

Question: Are you in the rut? Is your Church in the rut in regard to sowing the good seed?   Is it time to look for a new venture and a new field in which to sow?

*View of the rear of the chapel where visitors read the text and enter
the setting of the chapel adjacent to Mr Smith's kitchen*

During the early years from 1983 visitors always entered through the front door to the chapel. This was chronologically correct as they encountered the 1828 chapel before experiencing the 1914 schoolroom.   For this reason the 'replica' of Mr Smith's kitchen was situated right by the front door - as the kitchen was chronologically in use well before any chapel of course.

However at a later date an introductory audio-visual was made and placed within a model of Filey Ebenezer Chapel   Thus visitors were often invited to move on to the former school-room where it was more convenient to arrange seating with tables and offer the facility of a hot drink. However the point was still proudly made to these visitors: Mr Smith's kitchen came first - with 'chest of drawers pulpit' and drying washing hanging over the kitchen range!   This was where it started.

Hugh Bourne Card: Take Care of the Children

Hugh Bourne's father Joseph Bourne was a 'drunken violent man' and the home at Bemersley in which Hugh grew to adulthood was at times a totally unsuitable place in which to live. Hugh expressed his deep fear of 'being in hell before night' at the beginning of a day; he also spent the night with a 'fear of being in hell before the following morning'.

Alcohol was seen as the root cause and this firmly tipped the balance for Hugh in the direction of *total abstinence*. From his own experience of a miserable childhood he wanted no other child to suffer as he had done. The well-being of children especially was a strong driving factor in this crusade throughout his ministry in which he gave a firm emphasis to the importance of Sunday Schools and Total Abstinence.

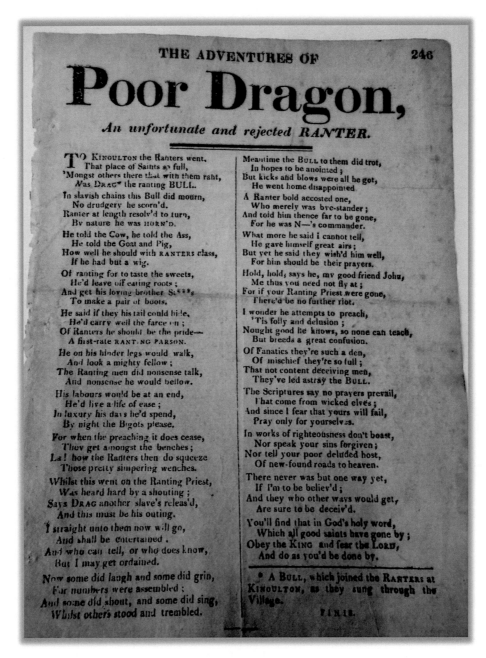

Poor Dragon
Opposition to Primitive Methodist Preaching

The event described took place in Kinoulton a small rural community approximately 8 miles to the south east of Nottingham. The early years of Primitive Methodist expansion in the East Midlands have been nicknamed 'The Ranter and Rotten Egg period', however this broadsheet takes the opposition to the Ranter preachers a stage further.

A bull is introduced to the situation. Whether this happened by deliberate intent or accident is not clear, however having happened the incident is not now to be ignored but recorded. Thus opposition to the Ranters is intensified by the ridicule of the verse, and the fact that the writer has gone to the trouble and expense of going into print to promote his view of 'true religion' to the members of his society who may now be wavering:

You'll find that in God's Holy Word, Which all good saints have gone by;
Obey the king and fear the Lord, And do as you'd be done by.

24

4) Mission with the Widest Remit (Book-sales)

Mark 5 vv.1-20 Jesus Visits Gentile Territory - The Healing of the Demoniac

Mark 5 v.15b: He was sitting there clothed and in his right mind; and they were all afraid.

This story is about Jesus moving beyond the safety of his own people to embark from the boat on to Gentile land, where he came face to face not just with a Gentile but one suffering from a serious mental health problem.   In the image of this one disordered man the mission of Jesus is summed up perfectly: God cares equally for all his children whether Jew or Gentile.   God cares equally for all his children whether they are of sound mind or of disordered mind.   In every case his desire for them is health, healing and wholeness.

The Englesea Brook project received substantial support from Connexional leadership over many years because it embodied the principle: 'For the many, not just for the few'. Here was mission with the widest possible remit.   Gratitude 'was' and 'is' deeply acknowledged: Thus the Minutes of the Englesea Brook Management Committee held 26 January 2001 read as follows:

a) The Barratt Trust has granted a sum of £10,000 pa for five years 2001-6.

b) The grant of the Chester and Stoke-on-Trent District will increase from £2,000 to £3,000 per annum.

c) The Fund for Home Mission will offer a sum of £1,500 per annum.

The Meeting expressed thanks to the Rev Dr Brian Powley and to Mr Alan Pimlot for arranging the grants.

In very few words a vast gratitude was expressed. These were substantial figures but it must also be noted that those at Englesea Brook who were in receipt of these grants were not just 'beggars', they were also 'workers'.   These 'workers' could not have worked harder - particularly when it came to shifting boxes of books around the country for book-sales. Those who drove the vans were equally to be applauded.   David Scott for instance who was the project's treasurer played a key role in driving the vans and counting and banking the money after the sales.   These were not small sums either - for instance in 2008 the total taken from all the book-sales run that year was £21,672.   The expenses were £5,265, leaving a balance to use of £16,407.   Those figures are typical of the annual book-sale turnover (7 Nov 2008).

Often church activities reach only church-minded people. Some of the 'community gatherings' held on church premises such as coffee mornings, luncheon clubs and concerts reach a wider adherent audience of those thought of as being on the 'community roll'. That is good, but book-sales reached a yet another much wider secular audience.   They reached those who were interested in reading popular books, those who were collectors of books on specialist themes and those who were looking for a bargain.   Book-sales reached beyond a community attracted by 'churchy' activities; book-sales reached into the secular world.

The sale of books where the books came from Methodist Ministers who had reached a point of retirement and who were needing to 'thin down' also definitely implied a theological / biblical theme in many cases. However those who had these specialist books often had quality books on other subjects as well.   Books in both these categories were the books that 'the world' queued up to view. When the doors were opened for the early book sales at Mow Cop there was a queue across the car park, up the hill and round the corner!

It is important not to claim too much, however it is believed that there are two valid points that can be made about what happened in this context of 'a book-sale':

1) Books that relate to the 'faith' are sometimes sold to those who do not as yet have 'faith' but who have an open mind and wish to discover more.

2) While coffee mornings and other social events often attract a preponderance of female visitors, book-sales attract men as well as women, and sometimes even a preponderance of men! It's quite an achievement to get men on to church premises - especially with so many books on spiritual themes laid out on the table for them to browse. However it happened!

Book-sales were a 'star in the crown' in relation to the making of Englesea Brook. Behind the scenes two people played a key role in making possible the book-sales. One was Pastor John Cumberbatch of the Kidsgrove Pentecostal Church who offered storage space for books on his premises.   Careful enquiry had been made within Methodism seeking an available room where books could be stored, sadly all had declined. John Cumberbatch and his congregation said 'Yes' and did so consistently over many years. The other star behind the scenes was Michael Dawson (usually known as Mike) who regularly made his car available to move books. While others feared for their springs, Mike said 'yes'. Again, very grateful thanks are expressed.

Further it wasn't necessary to have a theological training to collect books. A driving licence, ability to drive a van and the available time were the main requirements for the 'willing'.

It wasn't necessary to have had a marvellous education in order to move heavy boxes, sort books and arrange them on tables before the sale opened.   What was required was a strong heart, a good back and available time to spare.

It wasn't necessary to sell every book at any one sale. Some books that did not sell in one location would sell in another.   Some books were just far less likely to sell! However a change of venue with the same books, but also with the addition of further higher quality books always moved on some of the more resistant volumes.   A significant part of the money taken at any sale would come from quite a small number of higher-priced, higher-quality books. A smaller sum would be taken from the sale of a larger quantity of lower quality books.   However with skilful pricing the customer got a very good deal and Englesea Brook received a very handsome total sum.   Alan Rose is to be thanked particularly for his knowledge of books, his knowledge of the book-trade and his skill in pricing.

It wasn't 'automatic' that every book-sale would be highly successful. At Hanley in a room over the Methodist Book Centre the books were laid out.   The theory was that the customers for the new books in the shop below would also look upstairs at the second-hand. The theory was that with the usual advertising in the form of a 'news story' with the theme 'A New Location, New Books and New Opportunity' as a free advertisement in the local press - the public would roll in. Sadly they only trickled in! Having carried all those boxes of books up the stairs for the sale they then had to be carried back down at the end of the sale as well.

Chester Cathedral was disappointing as well. Here the agreement was that the cathedral should have 50% of the takings or that the book-sale should pay a rental of £10 per week. It was extremely generous of the cathedral to offer space for books at modest charge; however with regret it didn't make money and we needed in due course to pull out. The problems could have been anticipated: There was not enough space to lay out enough stock to satisfy enough customers - many left empty handed. Most visitors to the cathedral had come to see the cathedral and not to browse second-hand books! We hadn't got the right clientele. (2 Jan 2003, 23 Feb 2003)

However over the years a vast sum of money (a six figure sum in excess of a quarter of a million pounds) was raised for the development of Englesea Brook Chapel and Museum from book sales at Mow Cop, York, Birmingham, Poole, Sunderland and Oakhanger.

Initially book sales were viewed as a way of raising funds to renovate the very run-down chapel at Englesea Brook. The bright idea of 'saving the chapel' was the easy bit! But how would this renovation be financed? The answer that came in a flash was 'hold a second-hand book-sale!' That was another easy bit! However in the longer term those volunteers also discovered just how much hard work was involved - the physical movement of books from one place to another did become extremely 'wearying' with the passage of the hours.

This idea to 'hold a book sale' had come from York where a *Feed the Minds* book sale ran regularly in a disused Anglican Church at the bottom of Micklegate. Such a sale was never just about *the money*, it was also about *the books* and helping them to find a new home where they would again be treasured. These were *good books,* so just think of all the good that was also done through moving those books on to new owners! At Englesea Brook the new audience would include preachers looking for source material as well as dealers and members of the general public coming eagerly through the Chapel door to view.

One success led to another, so once the chapel had been fully restored it was recognised just how useful further funds raised from continuing book-sales could be. Thus ongoing book-sales became part of the annual income to be used in whatever way was best for the expansion of the project.

It was noted of course that there was a vast difference between York and Englesea Brook in relation to 'location'. St Martin-Cum-Gregory Church was on Micklegate, a very busy York street in a city to which visitors with time on their hands constantly flocked. Englesea Brook was a rural hamlet with no significant population and certainly with no significant number of visitors making a path to the door. How could such a sale at Englesea Brook be publicised? What might such publicity cost?

There was also no obvious population at Englesea Brook from which to draw books. Would there be those from further afield willing to give books? If so, how could such people be identified? How would such books be received? Methodist ministers on the eve of retirement might be thinning down their books. Would they be willing to give their books, and how saleable would these books be?

How would the books get to Englesea Brook? Even if those donating books travelled to Englesea Brook to deliver them who would be there to receive them?

The answer was of course to shape the 'bright idea' to the Englesea Brook context. If this project was to be successful it was recognised that the first step would be to co-ordinate the gathering of books and the getting of them to Englesea Brook. Further it was also recognised that this task would then require the need to ask for 'favours'. It wasn't just a case of 'giving' books - but also a case of 'collecting' books and 'transporting' books. This would be the key to it: Could book contacts be found around the country who would be willing to house books if brought to them? And would it then be possible to collect them all up?

However, wonderfully it all fell into place. Those who were willing to give books, those who were willing to store books and those who were willing to drive vans *were* discovered. The *Methodist Recorder* and the local press gave a lot of free coverage and 38 years ago the first book-sale held at Englesea Brook raised £1,000. That was a lot of money in 1984.

One of those involved was the Rev. Dr. William Parkes the superintendent minister of the Biddulph and Mow Cop circuit, and he suggested that much more space could be provided for a future sale at Mow Cop Chapel which was very much larger and with a considerable amount of little-used space. So the 1985 book-sale was held at Mow Cop Chapel and it continued there each August bank holiday weekend for many years to come.

Book-sale money was the new decisive factor. It was enough to make the difference and without it Englesea Brook Chapel as a 'twinkle in the eye' would just not have happened. Without it what would the chapel be today? It might be a ruin, it might be a store, it might be a workshop. With a burial under the floor of the chapel it was not judged suitable for conversion to a domestic dwelling at that time - but in the longer term who knows? Whatever Englesea Brook Chapel might have become it would not be remotely like the place that we now know.

The book-sale continued successfully at Mow Cop for many years, and this may have helped indirectly to bring some measure of new life to Mow Cop Chapel itself. The fact that the chapel was being used for a significant event each August bank holiday raised its profile and reminded people again of the significance of Mow Cop for the Primitive Methodist story. There was a renewed recognition of the significance of the open air meeting that was held on 31 May 1807 and on the very site where the chapel now stands.

In advance of the sale Alan Rose and Martin Rigg did a large amount of the pricing as both of them had an involvement in the trade. There was quite a skill in this - the aim being not to give books away but to price the better books at approximately half the trade selling price. This made books very attractive to the general public and also tempting to the professional book-sellers. To make sure that as much was sold as possible and that no-one missed out, the last day of the sale was always 'half the marked price'.

As the years went on it was possible to run a sale in more than one part of the country at the same time. It was also possible move books that had been at one sale directly to a pending sale in another part of the country without needing to go back to a central base to unload.

This saved on van costs and minimised handling. It worked as long as the core sale stock was 'refreshed' with additional books that had not been in an earlier sale anywhere else.

The use of Oakhanger Methodist Church which had the advantage of being on a busy road also worked well. Each Saturday the book-sale sign was put out, those in passing cars pulled on to the adjacent car park, jumped out, scanned the stock and went on their way. They may only have stayed for a few minutes but the takings for the day would usually be in the region of £200 (7, 14 Feb 2004, 20 Mar 2004). For instance during the late summer of 2004 the 'takings' from sales on six Saturdays at Oakhanger was a total of £1524.36p. In 2006 the money taken on five Saturdays in the autumn was £879.75 (4 Nov 2006) which could be seen as disappointing. However, it might not be a comparison of like with like - as from a summer peak the quality of the stock during the autumn was likely to reduce.

At Poole John Russell was already a convert to the value of book-sales and he had run several of his own for local good causes prior to becoming an enthusiast for Englesea Brook. However, when he heard about Englesea Brook he became part of the team and part of the network covered by van trips.

John Russell also had a network of charity shops that he visited regularly and who were often very happy to off-load stock. It might be thought that these would be low quality books that charity shops could not sell, so how could Englesea Brook? That would be erroneous thinking and for three reasons:
1) Charity Shops often receive more books than they can display or sell, however they do not wish to discourage those bringing books - the supply might then dry up. They need to continue to encourage the donors. It is better to have too many books than too few.
2) The Charity Shops will keep and display what they consider to be the best but that doesn't mean that there aren't other saleable books that remain and which they do not have space to display or keep. And who ultimately can judge what the public will buy? 'One man's meat is another man's poison'.
3) The books received by Charity Shops are substantially secular. Books received from retiring ministers are largely religious. Thus a broader range of books can greatly assist the sale and gain a wider range of customers when they are all laid out on tables at a book-sale.

Geoffrey Milburn at Sunderland also had some previous knowledge of book-sales. However when the needs of Englesea Brook became known to him he rapidly stepped up the pace of collecting and made that his main interest. He also helped with locally based sales. The van crew were well provided for as well, Mary Milburn put appetising food on the table for them - it was not just the offer of a drink.

Tribute should also be paid to those who did the clearing up afterwards as this was obviously the least pleasant and least popular part of the sale. Especial thanks are expressed to Mike and Georgina Harding who actually paid good money to take away a large part of the residue on numerous occasions (9 Jan 2008). The point here is that books which could not be sold in our sales could often be sold via the internet - but in many cases this would require a substantial 'wait'.

Question: Book-sales enlarged the scope of the outreach of the Englesea Brook project. Are there ways today in which we can enlarge the scope of our outreach and thereby enlarge the scope of our audience?

The Printing Press
Mission with a wide remit

The imprint of 'James Bourne, Bemersley' appears on Primitive Methodist publications from 1821. Thus in that year the imprint of 'Bemersley' appears on the *Magazine,* the *Minutes of Conference* and the *Hymnbook.* Previously the Bourne brothers had taken material for publication elsewhere including to *John Tregortha* at Tunstall.

In all probability the press or presses used at Bemersley from the 1820s have not survived. The press that is currently at Englesea Brook was used at Bemersley during the 1830s, and use of it for *Primitive Methodist purposes* was discontinued from 1843 as Primitive Methodist publishing was then moved to London. The Atlas Press now at Englesea Brook was rescued from Bemersley in the 1940s by a 'Stoke-on-Trent Printing Press Committee' and transferred to Hartley Victoria College, Manchester for safety. However the College closed and the press was then transferred to the Stoke-on-Trent City Museum before later reaching the final destination of Englesea Brook Chapel and Museum!

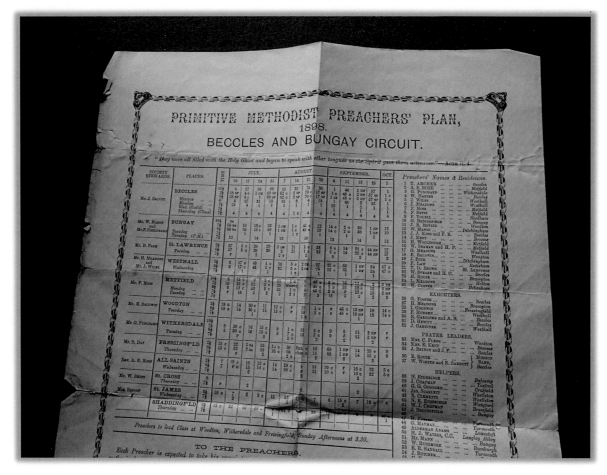

Beccles and Bungay Circuit Plan
Preaching to the widest possible audience

The circuit plan for this part of rural Suffolk shows preaching at a total of 12 places with the assistance of 25 Preachers, 7 Exhorters, 5 Prayer Leaders and 42 other Helpers. It has a personal significance to me as I spent the early years of my life aged 3-4 at Withersdale which is listed on the plan.

Class leaders are viewed as being particularly important, the instruction to them being:
The Class Leaders are affectionately requested to collect the Class Moneys weekly; to urge upon their members the necessity of active consecration to the service of God, and of support to his cause; to keep in view of our members their privilege of growing in the grace and in the knowledge of Christ.

This was a wonderful commitment from those preachers particularly who are listed. They had laboured on the land in many cases for six days of the week to eke out basic subsistence for themselves. However they did not then rest on the 'Sabbath'. Many of those listed then spent Sunday walking many miles to share the good news of the Gospel with scattered village congregations in East Suffolk.

Teaching to the widest possible child audience

This is an unusual plan… it's not a Preachers Plan. It also covers 15 weeks, not 13.   Each name has a number and each number has a date to which it is assigned between June 18th and September 24th. However just what is the role to which these people were being appointed each week?   That is not specified.

Further it is noticed that the time of the Sabbath School is 11.15 - presumably am.   Was this so timed to connect with a Sunday service? Probably, but it is also possible that if this was a large Sunday School with a number of classes and meeting on limited premises then it was timed to *avoid* Sunday morning worship!

The questions could be continued.   Certainly this plan seems to raise more questions than answers.   What *can* be said however is that the organisation shows a serious sense of purpose! For Primitive Methodists the work with children and with the achievement of the widest possible child audience was of the utmost importance.

5) Mission and Local Community (A Positive Response)

Mark 6 vv.1-6 - Trouble at Nazareth

Mark 6 v.3: Isn't he the carpenter, the son of Mary, and the brother of James, Joseph, Judas, and Simon? And so they rejected him.

The rejection of Jesus at Nazareth was a significant event. Whereas St. Mark gives just six verses in his summary account, St. Luke gives a much fuller picture in his fifteen verses (Luke 4 vv.16-30). The picture given by St. Luke highlights the biblical background - in the Old Israel prophets were rejected.   St. Luke also highlights the confidence of Jesus in the face of the mob 'He walked through the middle of the crowd and went his way' (Luke 4 v.30). Jesus had calmed the turbulent Sea of Galilee when disciples feared that they were about to perish (Mark 4 vv.35-41), similarly he calmed the turbulent mob.   It was sufficient to raise the question again 'What manner of Man is this?'

Jesus was rejected at Nazareth; John Wesley was rejected at Epworth and then limited when he returned to preaching from his father's tomb in the open air.   Similarly Hugh Bourne and William Clowes were rejected from Methodism because in broad terms they did not confirm to Wesleyan 'norms' - one of which in the early nineteenth century had become 'respectability'.

However why *specifically* were the Primitive Methodists rejected by the Wesleyans?   What were the grounds for Wesleyan rejection?   Was it partly the *wrong* Wesleyan travelling preachers in office at the wrong time? It should be noted that the invitation to return to the Wesleyan 'fold' came from the Wesleyans when new travelling preachers came into the Burslem Circuit!   However this invitation was turned down by the previously rejected group. They had found a new freedom, plus some success and they feared that if they returned the same could happen again when, perhaps, the next 'new' travelling preachers were appointed.

There was also rejection of the early Primitive Methodists by some in 'Society' - Mr Stephenson the Deist potter rode to Mow Cop on his horse to put a stop to the first camp meeting. However Hugh Bourne got the better of him and Mr Stephenson melted away. Hugh Bourne had in advance of the camp meeting walked to Lichfield to secure the license and thereby gain the permission which he believed would give him the advantage over his opponent.

So how did Connexional Methodism respond to the suggestion that the Englesea Brook Chapel might be saved and become a Heritage Centre that would present the Primitive Methodist story and Primitive Methodist values? The answer is that while a positive response was not generally expected for help to this 'run-down, back of beyond' small chapel in poor repair, nonetheless in this specific case the response could not have been better and to some was quite remarkable!

However reasons for this positive Connexional response can be seen as follows:
1) Already three Wesley/Wesleyan sites had been established (London, Bristol and Epworth) and it would be hard to justify outright rejection of the request for one similar Primitive Methodist site.

2) Primitive Methodist recognition was far more straight-forward than United Methodist (UM) recognition would have been. There would be a much greater difficulty with UM recognition as there were a number of separate movements in the 19thC which made up the United Methodist Church of 1907. The Methodist New Connexion, the Bible Christians and the, United Methodist Free Churches (UMFC) were the main component parts with UMFC itself also made up from a number of smaller groups. Primitive Methodism was straight-forward by way of comparison.

In the early 1980s, when the issue of the future of Englesea Brook Chapel arose, there was in many locations still far, far more chapel capacity than there were worshippers. In many communities Methodism was running many greatly under-utilized buildings and for pre-1932 reasons. The 'theory' of Methodist Union was that local societies would unite, new uses would be found for surplus buildings, and a new zeal for mission would be developed. Sadly in many places this had not happened. So it is not surprising that the redundant chapel in the hamlet of Englesea Brook, with a membership of 4 should be on the closure list.

Where Societies were uniting there also appeared to be another unwritten assumption in ex-Wesleyan minds as their premises were usually larger and better built. The assumption then continued that the ex-Primitive and ex-United Chapel would be the ones to close and the former Wesleyan Chapel would provide the new base. Sometimes the ex-Wesleyans also numbered more than the ex-Primitive and ex-United numbers added together, which drove the smaller bodies into a corner. 'Not over our dead body' was the response of the smaller Methodist Churches - 'we didn't know that closure was an integral and subsequent part of the deal!' So very often unions didn't take place from positions of strength but when weaker parties were forced into it. All was not well within Methodism.

Thus some would have argued that reviving the memory of Primitive Methodism to the point of establishing a Heritage Centre that spoke of the movement's worth was not a helpful step to take. Wesley was OK, and the Wesley sites were OK because they belonged to the whole of Methodism as that was during Wesley's life-time during the 18th Century. The petty squabbles of the 19th Century, as seen by some, would be best forgotten.

Of course these arguments can all be refuted and have been - but would anyone in a position of seniority within Methodism at that time have the courage to say so. Perhaps not - or perhaps not yet! How could an impact be made? The answer was: with the help of the *Methodist Recorder*. That paper carried an article on 14 April 1983 with the heading: 'Decision Time at Englesea Brook'. It made a mark connexionally as is evident from the subsequent correspondence in the *Methodist Recorder* and it gave encouragement to a group of young people from Wolstanton to set up a camp at Englesea Brook to begin to renovate the graveyard. A public meeting was held at Englesea Brook Chapel on Saturday 28 May 1983, 53 people attended and the movement to save the chapel and turn it into a heritage and outreach centre was launched. The Methodist Property Division then joined the conversation by asking how they could help, and from that time on their interest and support was outstanding.

Jesus was rejected by the community at Nazareth to the point of them seeking to deal violently with him (Luke 4 vv.28-30). So how would the quiet hamlet of Englesea Brook respond to a group of outsiders who wanted to make a new beginning at the Chapel? The answer is that it either bothered them so little that they never said a word, or that they were won for the cause.

Those who lived in close proximity to the chapel particularly wanted to help and there were plenty of opportunities for them to do so.

Four local people who had not previously been attenders at the Chapel joined a Sunday service when this was occasionally held. One near neighbour became a key holder and kept a look-out for any suspicious activity. Others from the hamlet came as volunteers to assist the leaders when large school groups started to arrive. When the educational programmes started there were at times sixty children on the premises and divided into a number of sub-groups for various activities. There was thus the need for plenty of willing volunteers.

This good relationship with the local community was also expressed as pastoral care was offered and received. Very occasionally there was a request for a baptism, a wedding or a funeral. On one occasion the local people collected £55 from among themselves as a gift for the chapel in memory of long-standing and much-loved local resident Miss May Swinnerton. On another occasion a gift of £1000 was made following bereavement. In 2004 a couple married in the chapel in 1954 returned to remake their vows. For all these people and others it was a very important spiritual home.

When plans were published for a new housing development just over the hill (Wychwood Park and with the possibility of further developments to follow) the chapel was again used as a public place for local residents to meet with local councillors and Rob Welsh from the planning office. In a 'small but beautiful' way Englesea Brook Chapel had become again a community hub.

Question: Jesus was rejected at Nazareth. Have you ever had a 'really good idea' that was rejected by others? Are there people within our congregations, or no longer within our congregations, who may feel rejected? What is there that is positive that we can do?

Are you ready for a ride on the Penny Farthing?

The image of the preacher with the penny farthing underlines the fact that Englesea Brook was never intended to be a museum of *passive* exhibits. Nor were visitors to be seen as those who were always 'viewers' and never 'participants'. Within the context of 'role-play' the child penny farthings helped the children to get to their circuit appointments more quickly than they would have done on foot (all within the length of the chapel drive, or later round the perimeter of the car park).

The tandem that was acquired was discovered to be extremely heavy and never ridden anywhere by adults or children! However it was 'good in theory' and made a good visual display.

Bicycles and tricycles were voted as 'first choice' for effective circuit ministry and these were loved by the children. Sometimes of course the preachers did need to have a lie down after a long bicycle ride to a remote chapel before going into the pulpit. They needed all their energy for taking the service, and for riding back!

The Mow Cop Community, by a local child artist

At the beginning of the 19thC, Mow Cop was considered by many to be a 'God-forsaken place'.

'Early in the year 1800 Hugh Bourne had purchased a quantity of timber at Dale's Green, between Harriseahead and Mow Cop, which circumstance brought him much into the neighbourhood; and at about the same time as he was prevailed upon to undertake the woodwork at the Stonetrough Colliery.… In this rough locality, 'The inhabitants were mostly uncultivated in their manners and unlovely in their moral character'.
(*History of the Primitive Methodist Connnexion*, John Petty (1864) p.10)

On 12 July 1801 Hugh Bourne preached in the open air at Harriseahead to a congregation that was too large to accommodate indoors. Later that year a chapel was built to accommodate 200 people.

There had been a ground-swell of activity in the Mow Cop area for several years before a camp meeting at Mow Cop was projected to 'counteract the evil influence of the Wakes' on 31 May 1807. The character of the Mow Cop hillside was already in transition and ready for more.

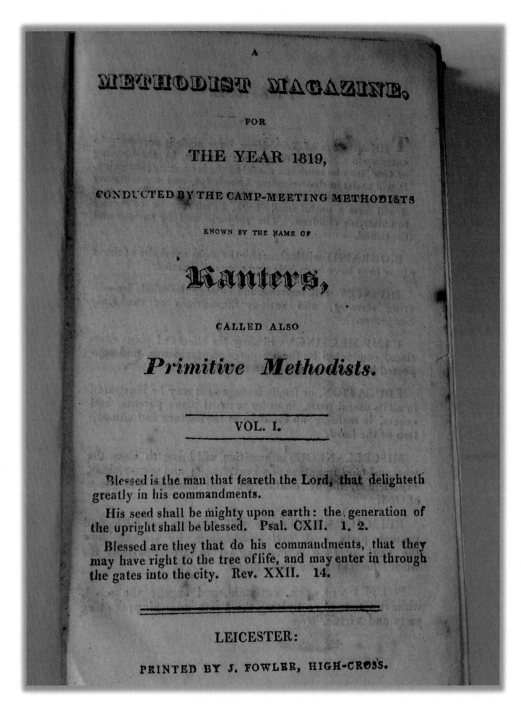

A Negative Nickname
They were called 'Ranters' as a term of abuse
Title page 1819/20 Magazine

The nickname *Ranters* like that of *Methodist* in the 18thC was not intended to be a term that flattered.   So why does Bourne use it on the title page of the monthly 1819/20 Primitive Methodist Magazine?

The term *Ranters* went back at least to the 17thC when the *Ranters* of that era gained a name for excess and a name of disrepute.   Surely that was the last thing that upright Hugh Bourne would wish for the Primitive Methodists!   Yes, indeed.   However Bourne used this title because he believed he had no choice: they were known as the *Ranters*.   There is the possibility of a curiosity value that he was also exploiting.   However Bourne will also drop the *Ranter* title as soon as he can.   The title of the 1821 Magazine simply reads *Primitive Methodist Magazine.*

6) Mission Through Food and Fellowship (A Welcome to All)

Mark 6 vv.30-44 - The Feeding of the Five Thousand

Mark 6 v.41a: Then Jesus took the five loaves and two fish, looked up to heaven, and gave thanks to God.

The large spiritual open air picnic known as the 'Feeding of the Five Thousand' is a pointer to the fact that food and fellowship belong together. That was a vast gathering but a similar point can be made from the story of the Last Supper (Mk14 vv.22-26): food and fellowship belong together.

Once a week when the museum closed to the public at 5.15pm volunteers on the premises stayed on. A few others arrived and sat with them in the museum making a circle. Hot drinks were provided and the sandwiches brought by each individual were unwrapped. Informal conversation was held until 6.00 pm when the bible study began. At 7.00 pm it concluded and after a few minutes of further conversation everyone went home.

On other occasions food was shared in the graveyard or in the chapel. Sandwiches were eaten by those sitting in the graveyard, or on the wall outside the chapel and on pews inside the chapel. Yes, it could be a bit messy at times, but it used the basic facilities that were available - and the fellowship was real. As one volunteer put it: 'End of season meals brought a wide range of people together, we shared fellowship having the meals in the pews; nothing overwhelmed us; nothing was too much trouble'

The 21st birthday since the beginning of the campaign to save the chapel was marked on Saturday 15 May 2004. From Chatwins bakery, a large square fruit cake decorated with an image of the chapel in royal icing was purchased at a cost of £96. This was cut into 100 pieces for the 21st birthday celebration (15 May 2004).

It should also be noted that in the Gospel story Jesus shared fellowship not just at a table but also at a well when he asked a Samaritan woman for a drink of water (John 4). The conversation was about the physical water 'in the well' and the spiritual water 'within the person' and which came directly from God. This 'living water' could spring up within a life and offer a much greater gift than the physical counterpart - the gift of 'eternal life' itself.

In Methodist circles today the 'cup of tea' serves a very similar purpose. It takes time to drink because it is too hot, and so the conversation begins. The conversation takes over and the half-drunk cup is now not very hot at all so it needs topping up to warm it up and the conversation begins all over again. This strategy of using a cup of tea as an ice-breaker worked wonderfully at Englesea Brook. When chocolate digestive biscuits were also available the 'feel good' factor was enhanced further.

It should also be recognised that the purchase of the seven virtual reality fames which were placed within the museum also enhanced the sense of fellowship and 'warmth' (5 Feb 2005, 10 April 2005, 2 May 2005).

The 'themes' of the flames were taken from John Ruskin's work *The Seven Lamps of Architecture.* The themes of these *Lamps* are: Obedience, Life, Power, Beauty, Truth, Memory and Sacrifice. Each of these words was linked at Englesea Brook with something within

Primitive Methodism and with the observation that these same themes were at work.

Obedience: This flame was adjacent to the window that contained the portrait of Hugh Bourne. He was a shy and diffident man who had grown up in a remote location and he never found public speaking easy. Yet he believed that he was called and did it, even though his reserve was such that he often spoke with a hand held in front of his face. He was obedient to the heavenly vision and God honoured his response. Thus *Obedience* was a large part of the motivation of Hugh Bourne. On two hard-boiled eggs and some dry bread he walked up to forty miles a day to spread the Christian message to as many as he could.

Life: This flame was similarly adjacent to the window that contained the portrait of William Clowes. The Gospel message came to 'life' for many when William Clowes was at hand. On display in an adjacent case his lantern can also be seen. He was thus a messenger of 'life and light' to many. Generally the early Primitive Methodist preachers sought to be 'burning and shining lights' within their communities. Having turned from a wild and rebellious youth himself, Clowes then undoubtedly became the most effective preacher within Primitive Methodism in offering 'life' to others.

Power: This was the biggest flame of all (4 feet in height) and it was positioned in the pulpit. The point was made that the preaching of the 'Word' can have a power that changes lives. Primitive Methodists did 'conversation preaching' as well as 'public preaching' and in both, power was displayed and lives changed.

Beauty: This was linked with the Ceramics case where love feast cups were on display. Part of a Victorian dinner service from a total of a hundred pieces and produced by Wood and Challinor of Burslem at the time of the Jubilee (c.1860) could also be viewed. Yes, Primitive Methodists did appreciate 'beauty' in the world around them, however their highest aim was to find 'beauty' in the transformation of human life.

Truth: This was the theme of the Missionary Case and included many artefacts from the Hodgson-Field Collection and kindly donated by Janet Field daughter of a Primitive Methodist Minister who went as a missionary to Eastern Nigeria. *Truth* related to the Missionary case. The call to be a missionary overseas was a call that could lead to the death of the missionaries involved. With Primitive Methodist Missions on the island of Fernando Po and in what is now Eastern Nigeria the risk was fully recognised. However they went.

Memory: Here the display was used to demonstrate the rich variety of Chapel Life within Primitive Methodism with: Camp Meetings, Processions with Banners and sometimes with a Band, Chapel Anniversaries, Sunday School Anniversaries, Sports Days, Outings and Feasts, Christian Endeavour Meetings and Rallies, Love-feasts, Watchnights and other Celebrations. *Memory* related to the rich tradition of Chapel Life

Sacrifice: This was linked with a Social and Political case. Here artefacts were used which illustrated the work of Primitive Methodist social reformers such as Joseph Capper, Joseph Arch and George Edwards. Farm labourers were put out of 'tied cottages' for Trade Union Activities. In consequence of his political activity, Joseph Capper the Chartist activist was imprisoned in Stafford jail. 'Principles' came with a cost.

The 'Feeding of the Five Thousand' is a story with a surprising outcome. Expectations were completely exceeded - has this ever happened to you?

Valued volunteers with a Lovefeast Cup

Margaret Holmes (left) and Madge Bennett (right), two valued volunteers over many years, are holding a Lovefeast Cup from Ellison Street Primitive Methodist Chapel, Jarrow.

The Lovefeast was of particular significance in early Primitive Methodism.   When a day of outreach was being held, the pattern of the activities would be to hold a camp meeting during the day in a public place, and then to retire for a Lovefeast - which would be held in a friendly farmer's barn in the evening. Just water would be offered from the cup and seedcake offered from the plate.   This was never intended to be an imitation of Holy Communion; it was rather based on the early Christian 'fellowship meal' the Agape, the 'breaking of bread', with the sharing of food together in close fellowship at the end of the day.

The particular cup that Margaret and Madge are holding is itself of significance because it is from Jarrow.   The stone built Primitive Methodist Chapel Ellison Street stood at the head of the circuit, it could seat 750 in the chapel and there were also seven ancillary rooms.   It had touched very many of those Jarrow lives - adult and child alike, with its claim for social righteousness. Indeed in 1936 many of those lives so touched were on the Jarrow hunger march to London.

Feed my Lambs

'Feed my lambs' (John 21vv.15-17) was a spiritual injunction found within the Gospel according to St John and taken most seriously by the Primitive Methodists. The picture makes the point in at least three ways:

1) The small banner to the top right of the picture is very direct. It simply says 'Feed my Lambs'.
2) The 'Sabbath School' banner from Buxton similarly makes the point: The Sabbath School existed for the purpose of teaching children.
3) The female preacher in the pulpit also makes the point. If she had not herself been taught as a child (and as a girl!) how could she now teach others?

Mr Smith's Kitchen

Mr Smith's kitchen was not just used for the preparation of food. It provided an opportunity for prayer and praise to be offered while real fellowship was built. It was here with the washing hanging overhead and with the kettle on the hob that they gathered.

Note that the kitchen range has an oven compartment to the right, a tap for hot water to the left, with the fire centrally placed and a kettle being heated. There are three flat-irons on the top of the stove and another kettle in waiting. In the corner stands the dolly tub with posser and wash board. The edge of the 'chest of drawers' pulpit can be seen to the right. This was where they met for fellowship, prayer and praise.

7) Mission Through Expanded Frontiers - Enlarging the Vision

Mark 7 vv.14-20   Beyond the 'Sacred'

Mark 7 v.18b: Nothing that goes into a person from the outside can make a person unclean, because it does not go into his heart but his stomach.

This passage points to a fundamental difference between Jesus and the Pharisees. The Pharisees were concerned with a correct ritual. In this case that was a ceremonial washing of hands when coming from the market place.   For Jesus what was most important was not an outward ritual but what was within the heart and mind of the person concerned.   This marked a deep divide.

Further Jesus then went on to the counter-offensive and pointed out to the Pharisees that despite their claim to righteousness, they were in fact in fundamental breach of one of the Ten Commandments. While the Commandments urged honour and respect for parents to be shown, the Pharisees had found a way round this.   They argued that if something was described as 'dedicated to God' then it could not be used to give help to a needy close relative.   Jesus reminded the legalists, with whom he was so often in conflict, of one of the Ten Commandments: 'Honour your father and your mother'.   They were guilty of setting the 'word of God' to one side in favour of their own 'man made traditions'.   What hypocrites they were! It must be recognised that actually the Pharisees were very well intentioned, but at the same time they were wrong. There is a major warning here - we can all make mistakes, while at the same time attempting to pursue what we see as the highest good!

The Chapel site at Englesea Brook received by the new management group in 1984 was seen as a potential 'fresh expression'.   Sadly the whole of the site including the two cottages was not available for this purpose as the decision had been made to sell the two cottages adjacent to the chapel to sitting tenants.   This brought a small gain for the Methodist Church with the addition of a little more added to the kitty for the building of the new Methodist Church at Wolstanton. Appeal from the Chapel campaigners (Alan Rose, Colin Dews and Stephen Hatcher) had been made to the Chester and Stoke-on-Trent District at the highest level to 'pause' the sale of the cottages, but this was to no avail.

The importance of the new building at Wolstanton was recognised by all parties, but it was still a fundamentally 'bad move' to sell the cottages to help fund it (one of which was sold for as little as £3,000), and deeply regretted for many years to come.   The new Wolstanton Methodist Church project gained only a little, but the task facing the Englesea Brook Chapel Appeal Committee was all the more momentous.   It also sparked the response from possible donors: Why, if you are now appealing for money for the chapel, did you sell the asset of the cottages for a knock down figure?   It doesn't make sense!

So responsibility by a *new Management Group* was taken for the chapel and what was left of the site after the sale of the cottages had taken place.   What was left comprised a narrow strip of land at the front of the former schoolroom and which tapered to the road.   There was also a drive that had shared access with the neighbour who lived on the other side of the chapel. There was just one parking space immediately in front of the chapel, but nowhere else. All other parking was road-side parking and on a narrow and twisting country road. There was also no land on either side of the chapel and the smallest amount at the rear which allowed access through the chapel to an outside toilet. .

Once essential renovation had been completed to the Chapel the Management Group knew that it was time to make the attraction far easier to visit in terms of access, and far more appealing to a much wider audience than the existing small group of highly committed enthusiasts. As the matter stood in 1983 only the really dedicated would visit. Additions to the site would need to be made over the years and it would mean both buying back and buying additionally. The years that followed on from 1983 would see the gain of the chapel drive with full rights for access and parking, the purchase of Brookside Cottage (£130,000), the purchase of land adjacent to the graveyard and the purchase back of 1 Chapel Cottages (£165,000).

The land that eventually became the car park for instance was offered for sale at auction with a guide price of £2,000. Every attempt was made to see if by offering the vendor Edward Whitfield what was considered to be a substantial sum it was possible to buy the land ahead of going to auction. (10 June 2002) This was all to no avail. Members of the Englesea Brook team went to the auction to bid with authority to even go to £10,000 to make sure that the plot was secured. Unfortunately the bidding went to £17,000 and the site was bought by a purchaser who believed that he would be able to build a house. The planners were quite clear that he couldn't, and had he taken the trouble to ask them before he made his bid he would never have purchased that land.

In due course Englesea Brook Chapel management were able to buy the land from the would-be builder - for £17,000 (9 Aug 2004). Brian Holt, surveyor then produced a report, and quotations were sought from contractors to make a car park (16 Aug 2004, 22 Sept 2004, report requested 6 Oct 2004).

Not only had an enormous sum of money been paid for a waste piece of land in a rural area, now another considerable sum was required to actually make it into a usable car park. The Methodist District produced £5000 with the assistance of the Rev David Westhead the District Property Officer; however there was still a step hill to climb and it was not until 2006 that the car park was actually ready for use (14 March 2006, 7 Sept 2006). It was certainly developed to maximum capacity as a car park, but also with space for 'visual aids' with three additional themes at the narrow tapering top end.

When visitors arrived to park they could easily have overlooked the grassed area at the slightly elevated end. However a substantial memorial to 'working children' had been placed to catch the eye. Having focused in that direction visitors would then see that there were seats for those who wanted to rest or reflect by the hedge and three crosses in front of the end fence. In addition there was also what looked like a grave at the centre of this area covered by a locked wooden lid. (The latter was for role-play when the Victorian child funeral took place.)

In 2008 this area was further enhanced with various seeds sown under the hedgerow. Included in this sowing were Cornflower, Corn Marigold, Black Merrick, Field Poppy and Corn Chamomile seeds (31 Dec 2008). This was to compliment the 482 Daffodil bulbs that had been planted in the grass and on the bank of the approach to the chapel on the other side of the road (8, 12 Dec 2008). In 2009 further enrichment took place with the purchase of 1000 Snowdrop bulbs and 1000 bluebell bulbs at a total cost of £315 (16 Aug 2009).

Back at the top end of the car park the visitors even at a glance would draw some conclusion - just from the three crosses. They would also discover that fuller interpretation of this area would be given once they were inside the museum.

(1) The stone was to commemorate 'working children' in the Victorian Age. These were real children and the circumstances of the death of these children and other details associated with the life of each of these children had been taken from the *Primitive Methodist Magazine.*

(2) The grave was to assist a role-play of a child Victorian funeral within a context of 'bereavement'. This part of the Victorian programme was only undertaken when specific discussion had been held beforehand with the class teacher(s). If a child in the class had recently experienced bereavement then it might not be appropriate and to err on the safe side the 'funeral experience' was not done. However on one occasion the request from the school was that it should specifically be done because a child in the class had recently been bereaved of a parent, and the school believed that for her it would be a positive experience. So that child joined in the funeral, talked about it afterwards and went home with her mind far, far more at peace than it had been since the death had occurred.

In the vast majority of cases and after careful discussion with the staff visiting it was agreed that the Victorian funeral could be helpful and it was done. The death of a Victorian child was a safe distance away from the lives of children today and there could be a degree of objectivity about it. The subject was always also raised with the children in advance so that they knew what was coming and discussed further after the role play had taken place.

Another example of how it was helpful is as follows. One of the boys present cried when the funeral took place and he felt embarrassed then when two of the others made fun of him for being such a baby. This could have been a very damaging experience, however one of the adult leaders present picked up what had happened, spoke to the boy most affected and helped him to understand that being upset was a very natural and positive response. This boy took the point and immediately felt far more confident. Later when the experience was discussed in class he volunteered to all the class that he had cried. This of course gave the teacher the opportunity to reinforce the fact that the expression of grief is a helpful experience when facing death.

Yes it was an area of considerable sensitivity but that doesn't mean that silence is appropriate either. If anyone is qualified to talk about 'death' it should include those within the Christian Church who in the real world come face to face with it with considerable regularity. The progressive marginalization of the Christian Church is seen within our society as the years go by. The numbers now attending Church and the age profile of those who do is now quite frightening. Maybe this is because the world doesn't think that the Church has much to say about matters of real importance. If that is so then the leaders and members of the Church have only themselves to blame.

Imaginative ideas at Englesea Brook were often picked up by the media, however the experience of the working-child funeral made it to the top. BBC Children's Newsround staff made a special visit from London to film the experience and give considerable space to it on their programme. While Church folk expressed their 'anxieties' the secular world saw the point and the benefit.   The experience reminds us of the continuing need for 'breadth of vision'.

(3) Thus three crosses to tell the Easter story and an adjacent 'graveyard' of just one grave covered with a lid stood at the top end of the car park. As has been indicated this grave served for the role play of the funeral of the Victorian working-class child.   It also served for the Easter story which was often linked with the Romans - thus targeting two school curriculum items - a Christian festival and the Romans in one school visit. A large white cloth was often placed beside the grave, and this assisted in the telling of the 'raised on the third day' part of the Easter story.

Question: On the physical plane drugs, drink and tobacco can each destroy life, and they are easy to identify. However human beings are mind, body and spirit - can you identify other enemies that may be at work and producing a similar result?

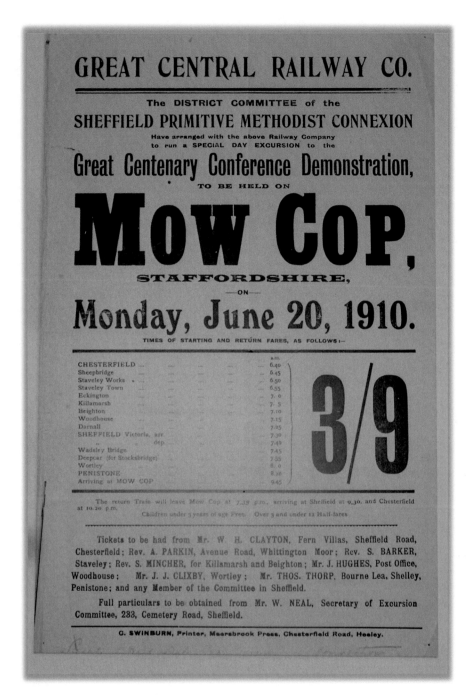

Mow Cop by train (1910)

The Great Central Railway Company offered a special one-day excursion to the Great Centenary Conference Demonstration which was to be held at Mow Cop on Monday June 20 1910. A return ticket was available for three shillings and nine pence whether travelling from Chesterfield, Sheffield or Penistone.

What the poster does not tell us of course is how many other special trains were running from other northern and midland towns and cities. This poster just relates to one Primitive Methodist District – the Sheffield District. What we don't know either is how the sidings nearer to Stoke-on-Trent coped with all those empty trains until it was time to go home again.

What we do also know is that the railway only took these visitors to the foot of a very steep hill. There was another mile to walk - and uphill all the way.

48

Filey Fisherman

Both banners are from Filey, and both focus on the care of the young. The smaller banner is from the Primary Department at Filey and this shows Jesus with children and welcoming children.

The larger banner shows an adult teaching a child - but what is the setting?   What is the language on the image?   One suggestion is that the picture is set in Egypt, and it shows Mary the mother of Jesus giving him instruction.   The environment may be unfamiliar, however nurture is centre stage.   Is this an imaginative interpretation of the 'Flight to Egypt' and what happened when they got there?

Use of the loud hailer by a member of the congregation at Mow Cop

As the fire lives by 'burning' so the church lives and grows by 'fishing'. Both of these images are 'pictures' and should not be pressed too far. Fire can destroy; fish when caught are often eaten! This is not the point!

The point is about the activity of those who are doing the fishing. They throw the net on one side of the boat and then catch nothing. However it doesn't make sense to then give up. It makes great sense to also throw it on the other side of the boat - especially when directed by a third party standing with a loud hailer on the shore. Church activities sometimes do 'more and more' for fewer and fewer people. That is not what God intends. The call is to throw the net, a large net, in a new direction. The invitation is for all..

8) Mission Through a Historic Site - Life on the Heights

Mark 9 vv.2-13 - The Transfiguration

Mark 9 v. 7: Then a cloud appeared and covered them with its shadow, and a voice came from the cloud, 'This is my own dear Son, listen to him!'

The story of the Transfiguration is one of the high points in the Gospel story. It is a 'high point' because Jesus took three of his disciples 'up a high mountain'. However it is also a high point because it is a prelude to the Resurrection that will be announced later in the Gospel story.

The appearance of two key Old Testament figures is very significant. Moses was the great Law -giver of the Ten Commandments and the Book of the Covenant (see Exodus 19 - 31 and especially Exodus 20 vv.1-17). Jesus himself was through his life and teaching the fulfilment of Old Testament Law, and the bringer of a New (Gospel) Law. Now love for God and love for neighbour summed up all that had gone before (see Matt 5 vv.17-20; Mark 12 vv.29-31).

Elijah was the great Old Testament prophet who had opposed Ahab, Jezebel and all the prophets of Baal. He had done so by inviting the 'opposition' to a high profile contest on Mount Carmel. All Israel was to know that the God of their fathers, and not the God of their current neighbours, was *the* true God.

With the religious teachers of his day whether Pharisee, Scribe or Sadducee, Jesus too entered into conflict. He too pointed to the God of their fathers rather than the God of their current religious teachers. He too would achieve ultimate 'victory' not just because the power of God would be at work through him, but because ultimately in his resurrection it would be more fully revealed 'He was God' (John 20 v.28: 'My Lord and my God').

Mission at Mow Cop. It was recognised from the beginning of the establishment of the Englesea Brook Heritage Centre that while Englesea Brook was a very significant early Primitive Methodist site with preaching from 1811, Mow Cop went back four years earlier to 1807. The 31st May 1807 was the significant date and Mow Cop was the most significant place.

However Mow Cop Chapel was not an 'offer on the table' as a heritage site. In the 1980s Mow Cop had a small congregation who were very traditional in outlook. The building was of considerable proportions and in very poor condition. It was not a suitable location for a 'fresh expression'. Englesea Brook was much the preferred choice. It was also available, Mow Cop wasn't.

However the book-sale established an early link with Mow Cop and this wasn't just over the weekend of the sale. Books were brought to the chapel site during the weeks before the sale, books were sorted and priced on the site, and there was also clearing up on the site afterwards. This gave contact with some of the Mow Cop members, an awareness of the state of the premises and some contact with the wider community over a number of weeks.

It was also clear that customers could find their way to Mow Cop, but not without a degree of traffic chaos in the vicinity of the chapel shortly before the book-sale was due to open on the first day. The volume of traffic lessened through-out the week to the greater satisfaction of the local residents. It was explained that the book-sale only happened once a year and the chapel was after all a public building. Primitive Street breathed again.

There was also a very positive side to this: Englesea Brook took approximately £2,500 at the first two day sale. Mow Cop Chapel received a generous donation from this and gained a lot of good publicity among those who were visiting. It was a place for bargain books and good quality refreshments. One bookseller described it as the 'best book-sale in the north of England'. In fact 'book-sales' meant that many more people now also knew where the chapel was situated! With black mould on the walls of the chapel it was also not difficult for visitors to see the parlous condition of this building. Similarly the size and age profile of the congregation was not such to offer vast hope for the future - resources were very limited.

Yet in their hearts this small congregation did want better even if in practical terms they did not know how to achieve it. They loved God and their Chapel very much, they were generous givers and they were prepared to move if someone would lead and show the way. In due course the afternoon service moved to a Sunday morning, a Mother and Toddler Group was commenced, weekly Bible study was held, pews were taken out and flexible seating was put in. Money from the sale of another chapel in the circuit was allocated to Mow Cop and this was sufficient to supply a new roof! Hallelujah! Little by little progress was made; little by little a corner was turned. A number of new people had now also joined.

With major upgrading Mow Cop also became a suitable site for school groups to visit when they were also visiting Englesea Brook. Mow Cop members received an immense emotional lift through property renewal and then again remembered things about themselves that they had almost forgotten when the future of the chapel had previously seemed so bleak. For instance the wooden cross hanging on the wall of the chapel had been made by German Prisoners of War during the 1940s. At the end of the war the then released prisoners offered it to their chaplain the Rev Joseph Howe, and he in turn offered it to Mow Cop Chapel when he was stationed there in the 1950s. Here was another part of the Mow Cop Chapel with a story to tell, and it was very appropriate to do so with 'handling' for the pupils when offering the 1940s/ WW2 programme to schools.

Over a period of 35 years transformation had taken place at Mow Cop Chapel and surely that was right. Given the will it would be 'right' in any chapel in any location, so how much more within the one that stands on the Primitive Methodist 'Mount of Transfiguration'.

It should also be noted that the annual open air celebration that was held near to the 'folly' at the summit did not just commemorate the early camp meetings. It also commemorated Mr Wesley and his 'field preaching'. Specifically on 8 June 2003, the Wesley Tercentenary service to mark the birth of John Wesley was in the form of an open air celebration and this was held at Mow Cop. The Grace Darling Singers led the Praise, and the three speakers were the Rev Gwyneth Owen, Mr John Bell and the Rev Dr Stephen Hatcher (8, 15 June 2003). At Chester Cathedral on Sunday 15 June the celebrations continued with the North Shropshire Methodist Youth Choir leading the Praise and with the Rev Dr Timothy Macquiban as the preacher.

In 2005 Alan Wood of the Stoke Cine and Video Society was invited to Mow Cop to film the event that included the North Shropshire Methodist Youth Choir with 4 blocks of lively and lusty singing of 8-9 minutes at a time. (23 May 2005, 10 Dec 2005).

Alan Wood continued to undertake filming each year as the bi-centenary approached. He also put the cine-film taken in 1948 of a large gathering at Mow Cop in May of that year on to video so that it could be used at Englesea Brook as part of the visitor experience. (2 Jan, 16 Feb 2008)

The whole ethos of the Mow Cop summit was such that it not only attracted pilgrims, it also attracted the media. For instance in 2006 Lamont Howie from Radio Stoke arranged for a small team to visit Mow Cop to record for the Sunday Programme which was scheduled for broadcast on the 4 June. The North Shropshire Methodist Youth Choir assembled, the loudspeakers were set up, the yellow jackets were put on as the crowd gathered and BBC Radio Stoke under the direction of Simon Penfold went into action (31 May 2006).

Of course even bigger celebrations took place in 2007. Royal recognition of the significance of 31 May 2007 took place on 11 May when HRH the Princess Royal visited the Potteries specifically for a special presentation at the Forum Lecture Theatre in the Potteries Museum and Art Gallery, Hanley. The highlight of this was sixty children in Victorian costume offering a short role-play of the Victorian working-class Sunday School. The New Victoria Theatre, Stoke -on-Trent under the direction of Peter Cheeseman had previously prepared its own slightly earlier successful documentary *Burning Mountain* about the early Primitive Methodists. Now before Princess Anne and other distinguished company in song and with drama the thirty minute presentation of the 'Primitives' unfolded. An actor from the New Victoria Theatre played the part of Hugh Bourne; however apart from that the whole of the production was both devised by and presented by the local Methodists.

The celebrations continued during 2007 in a number of ways but one of the most significant was the Open Air Celebration at Mow Cop with the President and Vice President of Conference and the North Shropshire Methodist Youth Choir. This was followed with 'Praise over 200 years' back in the Mow Cop Chapel at 5.00 pm - with copious cups of tea offered between the two services.

Nationally other events took place as well. For instance this same weekend the annual Pentecost Celebration was held at Cliff College. A paper was given on the theme of *Primitive Christianity* during the late morning and a Ranters' Service was led by the Rev Steve Wild in the marquee during the later afternoon.

On the 31 May the Rev David Leese and Mr Robert Higginson led a historic walk which finished with a Lovefeast at the former Wesleyan Mow Cop (Square) Chapel.

Historical banners that had at one time been carried down the street for the world to see were now permanently on display in Mow Cop Memorial Chapel. With all this activity Mow Cop Chapel itself was fortunately saved from closure - there had been a major upgrading of the premises and renewal of the congregation. Indeed the success of the display at Mow Cop led to a request from the Methodist Conference for a banner display there also. Thus the 2009 Conference asked if the banners could be loaned to further brighten the amazing 1930s Art Deco building in Wolverhampton where the Conference was to be held. The request made was - 'Please send your brightest and best banners' (7 Feb 2009).

Question: Have you ever had a 'mountain top experience'? In the physical world this could happen at Mow Cop, but what about the emotional and spiritual worlds of life? How have you fared there?

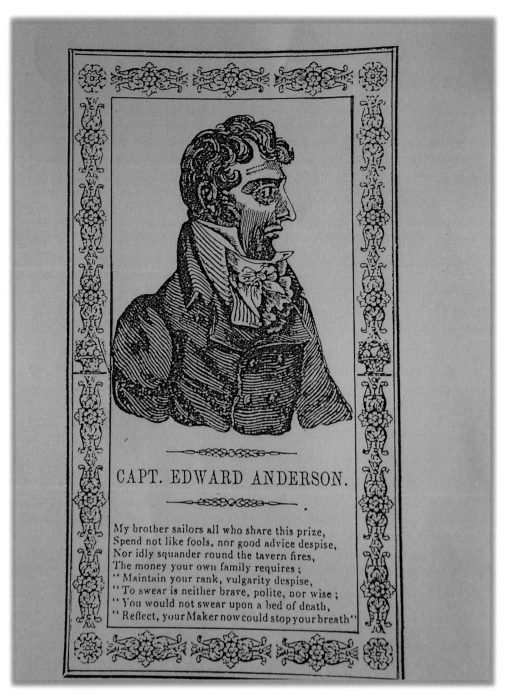

Captain Edward Anderson

Captain Edward Anderson took on a very significant role at the camp meeting at Mow Cop on 31 May 1807.   He hoisted a flag to show enquirers coming from a distance just where on the rocky hillside the 'camp meeting' was taking place.

The illustration shows a picture of the captain and the first eight lines of his poem addressed to his 'brother sailors'.   However even with a casual glance at the picture one cannot help noting that the picture appears to show someone of very fashionable dress!   Is not his dress incongruous with the verse that follows?   Certainly he was from a different world than Bourne and Clowes.

The plus side of course is that if he was dressed at Mow Cop as someone of 'standing' in the world, then this may have helped those gathered for the camp meeting to see off Mr Stephenson the Deist when he arrived on horse-back to object.   Captain Anderson could have been quite a plus!

Transfiguration

How is the 'Search the Scriptures' banner best interpreted? Three simple points can be made from the image that is presented:

1) The Bible is central to the Christian revelation. It is 'The Book of Life'.

2) The preacher is called to *elevate* the teaching that is contained therein.   This is illustrated by the pulpit cushion which is elevated above the earth and also appears above the clouds.

3) Divine illumination (from above) is required and is received.

The Mow Cop Chapel Pulpit

The pulpit is a symbol of Transfiguration and Transformation. However it does not stand alone.

Note the total setting at the front of the chapel which also includes a massive pipe organ. This is the direction in which the congregation will face. As they do so they will focus on both the preacher leading the worship, and the music (and choir) leading the singing.

However there is one more element of the utmost importance, the writing on the wall: 'Glory to God in the Highest'; 'On Earth Peace'; 'Goodwill toward Men.' Here are three themes of the Christian life (not one) and the total context and purpose of worship is summed up perfectly.

9) Mission Through a Domestic Dwelling (Brookside Cottage)

Mark 11 vv.1-11, 19; Mark 14 vv.3-9 – Bethany

Mark 11 v.19:   When evening came, Jesus and his disciples left the city.

Bethany, a village near to the Mount of Olives and two miles east of Jerusalem, was the home of Mary and Martha. (Mark 11 vv.1-11)   It was on the outskirts of where the action of Holy Week and Easter would take place, but also just far enough away from it to be a place for quiet thought and physical rest when Jesus needed it.   According to Saint Luke the Mount of Olives and its adjacent village Bethany was the base from which Jesus took two decisive actions.

There was action at the beginning of the final engagement with spiritual leaders at Jerusalem: 'As he came near Bethpage and Bethany at the Mount of Olives he sent two disciples ahead with these instructions; 'Go to the village there ahead of you; as you go in you will find a colt that has never been ridden. Untie it and bring it here'. (Mark 11 vv.1, 2)

Then when the action reached the final phase before the earthly Jesus left this physical world Bethany was also the last place where Jesus met with his disciples while still in earthly form: 'Then he led them out of the city as far as Bethany, where he raised his hands and blessed them. As he blessed them he departed from them and was taken up into heaven' (Luke 24 vv.50, 51).

Some visitors came regularly to Brookside Cottage because they similarly found the ambience helpful.   Englesea Brook was a quiet hamlet where the birds sang and the brook babbled. The cottage itself was compact, peaceful, and comfortable. However it was also modern and practical with a television inside and somewhere to park the car outside. Brookside provided real distance from the modern busy world and renewed the visitors with energy to go back and face that world.

Brookside Cottage offered a place for holiday, relaxation, retreat and study. Scholars and students alike who wanted to do serious study came to spend time in the cottage. Professor David Bebbington and Professor Robert Colls each spent a week in the cottage at different stages to research a chapter for a forthcoming book. The Rev Steven Wild a tutor at Cliff College came for a week to stay in the cottage with three senior students who were training to be evangelists.   Others came to write an article for a Journal, to prepare an address for a meeting or to find illustrations for a sermon. Brookside Cottage was a haven for those in need of spiritual refreshment. Within this cottage and at its heart was the library for the re-stimulation and renewal of the mind. For fuller information specifically about the library see chapter one of this work (Engaging Minds).

The pond with fish in the front garden added to the tranquillity, and the land at the rear offered plenty of space to hang out the washing and to park.   Two substantial sheds at the rear of the garden were used as storage space for the more bulky equipment required for the school programmes.   This included replica penny farthing bicycles for the children to see and often ride as part of the Victorian programme, and bicycles and tricycles for children to ride as part of the 1940s programme. The wheeled funeral bier was also kept in one of the sheds.

The cottage served a number of purposes that all related to the total mission of Englesea Brook Chapel and Museum. First of all it sometimes meant that during the week of the visit a relationship at depth was created between museum volunteers and the visitors. This was at a much deeper level than was possible on a single day visit to the museum.

Secondly it housed the library in a secure way, and yet kept it reasonably accessible. Yes, it would have been better in some ways if the library could have been housed at the main museum site for those making a day visit and undertaking research using the chapel premises. However the journey from the chapel to Brookside was only a two minute walk and the inconvenience to museum volunteers was not major. It meant that the front room of the cottage was put to good purpose. It meant that the library was very secure as that room was kept alarmed when not being legitimately accessed. It also meant that the cottage more than paid its way. After all bills had been paid the revenue even from the modest charge made for the accommodation was in surplus. (In the year 2006 for instance the cottage was let at a weekly rental from £75 to £145 according to the time of the season) This provided extra support for those parts of the chapel and museum that were more labour intensive and less financially productive.

Within very early Primitive Methodism the spiritually weary found 'refreshment' when at Old Jane Hall's cottage in Harriseahead they met together for prayer. At about the same time others in Tunstall found similar 'refreshment in Mr Smith's kitchen. Thus a powerful spiritual dynamic was created within these 'cottage meetings' and in due course this would overflow into the 'whole day's praying' at Mow Cop.

It should be noted that before Brookside came onto the market a serious attempt was made to buy Red Rose Cottage - and had this happened it would have offered much greater scope than would ever be possible at Brookside. This is how it happened, or more correctly- how it did not happen:

Although Brookside Cottage became a star in the crown it was firmly believed at that time that there was an even brighter star that would have greatly assisted the development of an even more secure future. The double-fronted Red Rose Cottage, slightly nearer to the chapel, would have been even better. It had substantially more rooms both on the ground floor and upstairs within the main cottage building, plus significant out-building space at the rear in the form of a double storey outrigger giving another four rooms. There was also a small paddock. The imagination of those of us viewing the property and making the plans worked overtime. The asking price was £185,000 and the District and the Connexion both indicated support. What could possibly go wrong! The Chapel offer was also the highest bid received; however the vendors chose to accept a lower offer and Red Rose Cottage was sold elsewhere. It was feared by the vendors (who would continue to live in an adjacent property) that if children came to the premises then children would bring 'noise'. Englesea Brook was a peaceful hamlet and the sound of children at play to them would have been an intrusion. So Brookside Cottage became the fall-back with many working hard and long to raise £130,000 to buy it, to expand the project and make the whole operation significantly more viable.

At Englesea Brook before Brookside and 1 Chapel Cottage were purchased no attempt was ever made to replicate early cottage meetings. However the sense of fellowship within the weekly Bible study group members who met in the former schoolroom (now the main museum room), for the sharing of food and Bible study, was remarkable. This activity was probably that which was the closest to the experience within Mr Smith's kitchen two hundred years earlier. It is worth noting that the loyalty of the various members to that group which included Sue Frost a most enthusiastic worker was phenomenal; it was as if no-one wished to miss a minute of what was taking place. Spiritual hunger really was fed.

On site the significance of the cottage kitchen was further and fully recognised as of great importance within early history of Primitive Methodism. This was with the creation of a 'replica' of Mr Smith's kitchen at the rear of the Chapel. It should also be noted that the rear of the chapel is also adjacent to the front door, and this was part of the plan. This was significant and was intended to be. Visitors arriving came in through the front door and saw first of all - Mr Smith's kitchen. It was there right in front of them. In fact the visitor's book that they would sign was on the 'chest of drawers pulpit' which two hundred years earlier had stood in the real Mr Smith's kitchen. To complete the effect there was a kitchen range, a kettle and a pulley with washing hanging up to dry.

The subsequent purchase (or purchase back!) of 1 Chapel Cottage also brought great benefits by enlarging the space available and upgrading the kitchen. Previously kitchen facilities had been very inadequate so the purchase of 1 Chapel Cottage just next door immediately took pressure off the chapel/museum part of the site and gave space both for the preparation of refreshments but also their consumption. The front room of the cottage provided an excellent room for meetings and also a relaxing place for those to sit who wanted to drink tea or coffee. Office space moved upstairs to one of the bedrooms. The additional land gained with the purchase of the cottage was also a bonus especially as there was so little land at the back of the chapel. When schools were visiting, the rear of 1 Chapel Cottage served for skittles and skipping, and the drive served for hoops.

Question: From cottage to cathedral, God can be found. Where do you find him most? What is the implication of this for Mission?

'Bethany'

A number of schools participated in the banner making project. Of these two particularly notable contributions were made as follows: One was a banner showing the work of children from St Mary's Roman Catholic School. The theme was: bio-diversity within the harmony of creation, and the need for a place of safety. Noah's Ark was such for the animals who were gathered within its walls. The other from Springhead School, Talke Pits showed 'diversity' within the security of the community in which they lived.

Bethany was a place of security for Jesus and his disciples as they faced the uncertainty of an increasingly unknown but hostile world. They needed the safety of a home a little distance away from the threatening city of Jerusalem.

Many who came to stay found that Brookside Cottage was similarly their *Bethany*.

The Primitive Methodist dinner service

The Primitive Methodist dinner service prepared for the celebration of the Jubilee (1857-60) would have been large enough to supply the needs of the historic Jesus and his disciples plus an assortment of 'publicans and sinners' - who were drawn to his loving, forgiving and hence magnetic personality.

However it must be remembered that when this Jubilee dinner service was commissioned by the Primitive Methodists the aim was not to put it in a glass case. It was intended to facilitate a 'fellowship' as real to the participants as that experienced by the first disciples.

The Dinner Plate which is part of a Dinner Service with over 100 pieces
The table is large and full - all are invited

The dinner service was purchased from Denmark in the late 1970s. At the time of the sale it was in the hands of a Danish artist who had inherited it from his forebears, one of whom had been a sea captain. From time to time this captain made the crossing from Denmark to the port of Hull in the UK and it was there that the sea captain purchased the dinner service. One can only make conjecture about the reasons behind this purchase: Had he seen the Primitive Methodists in action in Hull? Had he been impressed by the growing number of Primitive Methodist Chapels with their congregations of working people? Had he established a Primitive Methodist friendship or even commitment? Whatever the reason there was sufficient motivation for him to take a dinner service with just over 100 pieces back to Denmark on his return journey.

10) Mission with a Standard of Excellence - Grants and Trophies

Mark 10 vv.35-45 James and John Came Seeking an Award

Mark 10 v.43b: If one of you wants to be great, he must be the servant of the rest.

James and John came seeking a reward. However discipleship is not of that nature.   If an award comes to a Christian it is a bonus.

The mistaken request of James and John for 'favour' and 'glory' when Jesus came into his kingdom (vv.35-45) is deliberately set amidst passages of very different character within the closing chapters of St. Mark as Jesus makes his journey to the Cross. Thus in chapter 10 Jesus sets out some of the 'values' of the *hard* way which leads to the cross.   These are the following:

No easy divorce, the faithful route of marriage is a hard way too (vv.1-12).

Attach the highest value to children - they are the essence of God's Kingdom (vv.13-16).

How hard it is for those who have riches to enter God's Kingdom - it's not impossible, but it's certainly a very big challenge (vv.17-31).

Discipleship is about being a servant, even a slave, it's definitely not about 'glory' (v.43).

Before detailing the 'Awards and Trophies' that were received at Englesea Brook it is vital to note that apart from the faithful and enthusiastic support of 'volunteers' very little of this would have happened. Such volunteers fall into two categories: There were those who looked after the premises; there were those who interfaced with visitors including schools. Both groups are to be heartily thanked, and especially those who behind the scenes made sure that the premises were clean and tidy for the next day of opening.

At an early stage Marjorie Cookson undertook the cleaning of the premises and her husband Derek undertook keeping the graveyard tidy.   In fact the work on the graveyard could never be adequately done if just in the hands of one volunteer - there were broken down walls that needed a builder to repair for instance! However Marjorie and Derek did what they possibly could and did it with a cheerful spirit, giving an example both to those other volunteers who were there then and to those who would follow.

Of course grants from the Methodist Church and from Museums Libraries and Archives (MLA) were given in expectation of achievement. Both of these organisations were interested in 'spreading the net more widely' to encourage more visitors generally and more schools to come on board for the education programmes at Englesea Brook. They were not disappointed, however the route by which this was achieved was 'faithful service'; this was not a route for 'glory-seekers'.

On one occasion Englesea Brook won the Cheshire 'Visitors' Choice Award' out of a total of twenty-two entries (13 Jan 2008) and twice it won the Cheshire Show award for the best attraction - an enactment of the Victorian Sunday School experience with Margaret Veal in role as the teacher. With this level of achievement both the Church and secular bodies would feel at ease about continuing to invest.

The banners at Englesea Brook and Mow Cop served to underline the high profile that the Chapel communities gave to their congregations generally and their young people specifically when they took to the streets in procession with 'banners bright'. In 2007 Margaret Veal began a special programme 'Explore the Hidden Depths of our Banners' (21 Feb 2008). The aim was for primary school children to engage with adults who were two or three generations older and for the children to find out all that they could about 'Banners, Processions and Whit Walks' that these now elderly folk remembered from when they were in their youth.

One of the schools taking part was St Mary's Roman Catholic School, Crewe. Contact from the school was made with a lady called Pauline Ollier and she 'remembered' as follows:

Dear children of class 4,
I have never carried or made a banner, but I will tell you what I remember about the banner that was in my Sunday School at Henry Street Methodist Church in Crewe. The Banner was usually in the school room but when we had a Carnival each August the banner was carried at the front of the procession. Banners were also carried when there were large open air meetings of different Methodist churches - so that people would know who was attending.
My brother did carry the banner and it was a very great honour, but as it was a very windy day it was very hard work. The banner got heavier and heavier as the wind blew harder and harder. I do remember sitting in Sunday School looking at the banner which was very brightly coloured and seeing Jesus who looked so happy with a little lamb in his arms.
I hope you enjoy making your banner and learning about them.
Yours sincerely,
Pauline Ollier

The 2008 Grant from *Museums Libraries and Archives* was given specifically to work with 3 schools on the theme of 'Cheshire in Bloom' at Englesea Brook. The aim was to make: A Memorial Garden to Working Children. This would be an attractive feature in itself with a wealth of wild flowers plus the pollinators that would be attracted. This care of creation in the small corner of Englesea Brook could be used as a teaching aid to encourage 'care of creation' throughout the Developed and the Developing World today.

On the 17 Jan 2008 contact made with a seed merchant for wild flower seeds to sow on the perimeter of the car park - partly under and partly adjacent to the hedge. Turf was also ordered and laid at the top end of the car park and this also provided a better setting for the grave of the working-child funeral.

This grave had been prepared two years earlier with work beginning on 22 June 2006. It had been made 5 feet long by 2 feet wide so that this would comfortably take the coffin which was 4 feet 6ins long and 18 inches wide. It was ready for the first 'poor child funeral' with a role-play of burial when Weston Coyney Primary School visited on 30 November 2006.

Question: How do we judge those whom we meet, is it by what they 'have' or by what they 'are'? How do we see ourselves in a 'servant role' today?

Plaques to the 'Great and the Good'

The *great* and the *good* within the Primitive Methodist movement were often remembered within the chapel and its congregation long after they had exchanged 'life' for 'immortality'. The three similar plaques on the bottom row of the picture are from Cardigan Road Primitive Methodist Chapel Leeds. The best known of those remembered here is William Beckworth JP a leading layman within Primitive Methodism and writer of a substantial account of Primitive Methodism in Leeds.

The plaque to Sir George Green JP from Scotland also underlines the distinguished public service given by a Primitive Methodist layman in the late 19thC / early 20thC.

Sir William P Hartley

Along with Sir George Green, a Primitive Methodist in Scotland, to whom reference has just been made, Sir William P Hartley was the other known (and much better known today) Primitive Methodist to have received a knighthood.

With jam making that started in a Colne kitchen, 'Hartley' would become a household name known and respected throughout the UK and beyond.   Sir William P Hartley (as he became) rose through the 'ranks' of society, but he never forgot the Church that had nurtured him. Many chapel building projects received from his beneficence as of course did Hartley College, Alexandra Park Road, Manchester.   Under the direction of Professor A S Peake the Primitive Methodists achieved in the 20thC a training that was 'second to none' in a building of similar high quality.

Children and Mission Van at Edlington Colliery
Major work with children in a great variety of ways was the greatest reward

The picture shows a Primitive Methodist Mission Van which has been taken by a horse to a specific location where it was believed that there was an important work to be done, in this case with children at Edlington Colliery near Doncaster. The memory they received would last a lifetime.

If nationally a comparative ratio of *adult membership numbers* to numbers of children with whom engagement was made is undertaken in the various denominations - then the Primitive Methodists excelled with the very substantial number of children with whom they engaged in relation to the total size of that denomination.

This van would have carried a staff of two or three young men who would live and sleep in the van and discover that Christian service 'Primitive style' was tough and demanding. If any of these young men had felt a call to the ministry believing that it was a soft number, a few weeks on the Mission Van led them to think again. The wooden van did have a stove for cooking and for warmth, but the temptation to try to keep it in overnight was to be firmly resisted. If the wind changed in the night and the stove got out of hand the preachers might find that they were fleeing from the Mission Van in their pyjamas.

11) Mission with Multi-Media Dimensions (Engagement with all the Senses)

Mark 11 vv.1-11 - Palm Sunday

Mark 11 v.5b: Some of the bystanders asked them, 'What are you doing, untying that colt?'

Jesus believed in 'visual aids' and he had demonstrated this throughout his ministry. Thus Jesus 'set a little child in their midst'; Jesus said 'Look a sower went out to sow' as he pointed to activity in an adjacent field; Jesus asked 'Whose head and inscription is this?' as he was handed a Roman coin. During the whole of his public ministry Jesus had used visual aids to good effect. Therefore it is not surprising that as he comes to the climax of that ministry he should continue to employ this well-tried method of gaining attention and making a point.

Thus on Palm Sunday - Jesus rode a donkey into Jerusalem for all to see. This was absolutely within the public eye (Mark 11vv.1-11).

The Cleansing of the Temple which followed (Mark 11 vv.15-18) was then seen as an assault on national religion and vested interest by an angry young man. News of such action would spread like wildfire. The reaction: 'How dare he?' spread through the pillars of rectitude and the wider public alike.

The anointing at Bethany (Mark 14 vv. 3-9) shocked at least Judas and he spoke out. But what we don't know is what the other disciples were thinking. Once Jesus had said, 'Foxes have holes and the birds of the air have nests, but the Son of Man has nowhere to lay his head'. How did this indulgence tie in with the teaching of a lifetime that he had given? It did and it did so vividly because in accepting the action Jesus was also accepting the woman who was making the action. To have declined the action would have been to decline her also. It was a vivid three dimensional event - he accepted the gift and he accepted the woman. But not all saw it that way.

Jesus ate the Passover Meal with his Disciples. This was yet another three dimensional event with food and drink plus words and action. (Mark 14 vv.12-25)

Indeed the events of Easter week are all multi-media from Palm Sunday with a donkey (Mark 11 v.1-11) to the Cleansing of the Temple (Mark 11v.15-18) to the Anointing at Bethany to the Last Supper (Mark 14 vv.12-25) and on to the Cross and Easter Day with an empty tomb. They engage with the eye-gate as well as the ear-gate, they raise questions that require answers and they invite the spectator to become a participant.

In the same way a visit to Englesea Brook has always appealed through the eye-gate as well as the ear-gate. It was never intended that it should be a 'boring museum' with only objects from a remote world viewed within glass cases. It was always intended that it should be three dimensional and invite participation. The curiosity of the spectator is to be stimulated, an invitation to make choices is extended and the visitor then becomes a part of the story.
Thus back in the 1990s an audio-visual introduction was made under the auspices of Manchester

Metropolitan University and offered to the museum as a gift. The equipment to play the tape thus produced was housed within the model of Filey Ebenezer Chapel. So when visitors arrived the doors of the Chapel were opened by the person on duty, the green button was pressed and an introduction to Primitive Methodism, Englesea Brook and the Museum Collection was given - as far as that could be done within eight minutes!

Over the years good links were established with the very early former Primitive Methodist Chapel at Wirksworth where the minister at that time was Martin Williams. This had happened naturally because Margaret Gleave a volunteer at Englesea Brook had a close link with Rosemary Dale a friend at Wirksworth. Some members of the Wirksworth congregation had also moved to Crewe and from there had become engaged at Englesea Brook as volunteers (Madge Bennett, Helen Prevett)

There was also a pulpit at Wirksworth that was used by female preacher Elizabeth Evans who was immortalised by George Elliot in *Adam Bede.* As Hugh Bourne had worked with Elizabeth Evans and as he was a great believer in female preachers there was a natural link with Primitive Methodism and in consequence with Englesea Brook. So Englesea Brook acquired the pulpit and this now proudly stands on site within the Museum.

However this link with Wirksworth sparked another link in addition - 'well-dressing'. Well-dressing was a long-established custom in Derbyshire and in parts of Staffordshire. So why not have a well-dressing at Englesea Brook - and of Elizabeth Evans - a beacon for early female preaching. Under the direction of Rosemary Dale and Margaret Gleave the making of the 'jig-saw' using flower petals of various colours, shapes and sizes was built up into a portrait of Elizabeth Evans. As can be imagined the colour in the petals did fade, but for a few weeks it was a remarkable exhibit and major attraction standing on the chapel frontage so that it could be seen by all, whether the museum was open or not. (13 April 2002, 20 July 2002)

Some-time later during the week beginning Mon 13 June 2005 Well Dressing took place at Englesea Brook with engagement from a number of schools: Richard Heathcote (14 June), Castle, Mow Cop (15 June), Silverdale St Luke's (16 June), Knutton (17 June), Mill Hill (20 June), years 3/4 Chesterton (21 June), years 4/5 Chesterton (22 June), years 5/6 Chesterton (23 June), Weston Coyney (24 June).

The bi-centenary of the movement in 2007 meant that this would be an impressive year! Thus in 2008 Englesea Brook reported to Synod the success of the 2007 Celebrations and the variety of ways in which the engagement had taken place. Among the activities included were the following eight achievements engaging the ear and eye 'gate', involving the screen and the 'person' and with promise for 'today' and 'tomorrow' (13-14 Jan 2008):

1) A personal appearance and engagement by a member of the Royal family - HRH The Princess Royal.

2) The Open Air celebration at Mow Cop attended by over 1000 people in the freezing cold and addressed by the President and Vice-President of the Methodist Conference.

3) The 'Ranter Preachers' making an Eggheads television appearance.

4) The 'Visitor Choice Award' for South Cheshire (First out of 22 entries)

5) The Award of a significant Grant from MLA (Museums, Libraries and Archives) to work specifically on the garden project for 'Cheshire in Bloom'.

6) The Gift of the Hodgson-Field Collection, the result of a lifetime's collection of ceramics by Janet and Bill Field.   The collection also includes artefacts etc. from the time that Janet's parents served as missionaries in Eastern Nigeria.   (Some of Janet's own experiences on the mission field as the child of Primitive Methodist Missionary parents were also recorded on the handsets.)

7) The restoration of the 1828 Silsden Organ by Derek Shuttleworth, organ builder, to become a working museum exhibit.

8) The step up from 'Registration' of Englesea Brook as a Museum with MLA achieved in the year 2000 to 'Accreditation' - a much higher standard.

It would also be the aim in the future for Englesea Brook to not be like a book that can be closed and put down.   The aim would be to raise new questions while giving answers to earlier questions!   It would be to 'whet the appetite for more'.

A *City Children and Country Ways* disc produced with the help of Prof. Stella Mills at Staffordshire University demonstrated further the breadth of the 'experience' that was available at Englesea Brook.

Question: Motives are easily misunderstood. In the Palm Sunday story both the bystanders and the crowds misunderstood what was happening. Are Christians misunderstood today? If so how? Does it matter?

The Magic Lantern

It was during the week before his death that Jesus went into *overdrive* with actions as well as words to make his point and to make his offer of a coming Kingdom.

The 'deeds' included the 'Cursing of the Fig Tree', 'Riding on a Donkey' on Palm Sunday, and 'Dying on a Cross' on Good Friday.   It was all highly visual.

Similarly the Primitive Methodists believed in the 'eye-gate' as well as the 'ear-gate'. This is clearly illustrated with their banners and processions outside.   The 'visual' as well was the 'spoken' was equally in use inside - for instance with the Magic Lantern that produced images on the wall.   It didn't *move* and it didn't *talk;* however it was still one of the wonders of the Victorian world when pictures were produced to match the words that were being spoken.

The Magic Rope Trick

In the picture the Rev David Leese demonstrates that things are not always what they appear. How can what clearly appeared to be one rope now have now divided itself into several parts? The answer is that what the eye has seen is not the whole story. With the use of only one of our senses we may be mistaken. Fortunately God has given us a number of senses and a mind in which to store past memories. The Resurrection which is at the heart of the Christian faith for instance is not a 'conjuring trick with bones' - a point made by a former Bishop of Durham on one occasion. Thus the fullness of the Christian life depends on a number of different dimensions. It is the revelation of God. It is also the response of the believer with critical mind, loving heart and obedient will. Response with just one of these alone falls short.

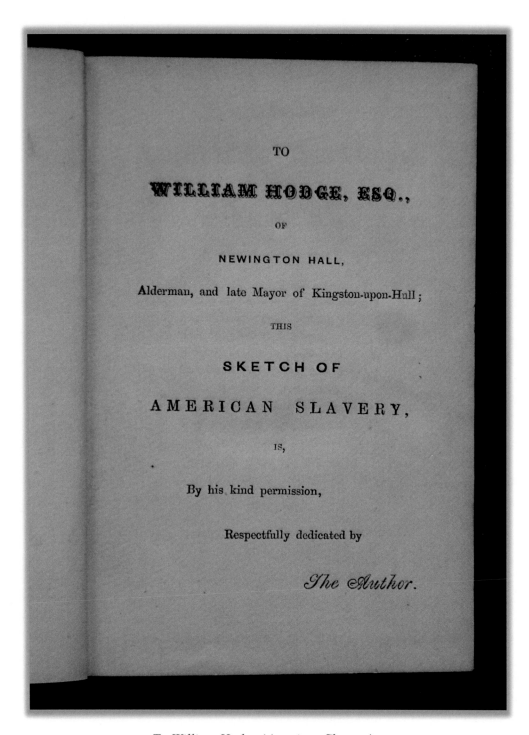

To William Hodge 'American Slavery'

The publication of *American Slavery* by the Primitive Methodists in 1862 and dedicated to Alderman William Hodge - a Primitive Methodist Lord Mayor in Hull at that time illustrates three things:

i) Primitive Methodist interest was in the whole of life and not just in the spiritual.
ii) A Primitive Methodist itinerant in the UK was sufficiently interested in *American* Slavery to write a book about it.
iii) William Hodge a Primitive Methodist who was also Lord Mayor of Hull, was fully in support of the campaign to grant American slaves their freedom and the book was thus dedicated to him.

12) Mission that is Universal and Eternal!   (The Widest Possible Vision)

Mark 16 vv.1-20 - Life over Death

Mark 16 v. 8a: So they went out and ran from the tomb distressed and terrified.

The Gospel story concludes in Mark 16 in three distinct sections of which the first section vv.1-8 is common to all manuscripts.   The Gospel then continues either with vv. 9-20, or with different alternative verses for verses 9-10.   Most Bibles print the whole of the text and it is listed as follows:

The Resurrection vv.1-8

An old ending of the Gospel vv. 9-20

Another old ending vv. 9-10

It is suggested that the fuller text for Mark's original ending was lost at a very early stage - perhaps during persecution under Nero (c. AD 64) or Domitian (c. AD 96).   What is quite clear is that even without the lost ending (and even if there was nothing after verse 8), the Gospel proclaims the 'Resurrection'.

Englesea Brook Chapel had been through a 'death and resurrection' experience. Numbers had been very low for many years, income had been low and in consequence little maintenance had been done. It was a vicious circle - a building evidently falling into disrepair is unlikely to attract new participants.   So the vicious circle continued and by 1983 the number of members had dropped to 4.   The age profile was not encouraging either.

However over the years since that 'tipping point' in 1983 the situation has been transformed. Visitors from all around the country and beyond started to ask if they could book in for a visit. These visitors were not all just devout dyed-in-the-wool Methodists either, nor just from 'round the corner' - for instance on 11 June 1997 George Pace brought a Heritage Tour all the way from St Helier, Jersey to Englesea Brook.

From the autumn of 1996 the promotion of the *Englesea Brook message* was taken off-site as well as on-site.   Services with an *Englesea Brook dimension* were taken in many different Churches and Circuits within the Chester and Stoke-on-Trent District throughout the year. This was given a particular emphasis during the autumn and winter of 1996 and the spring of 1997. Then of course Englesea Brook opened for the new season and with Sunday opening at Englesea Brook there was less scope for circuit preaching. Later the work was far more established and paid workers were used to cover duty on a Sunday.   Dennis Cornes, Ron and Bronwen Maddran and John Taylor are all fondly remembered for their Sunday afternoon term of duty.   When it was then possible to offer 'Sunday preaching' the circuits of the Chester and Stoke-on-Trent Methodist District responded with enthusiasm to the thought that this was also without charge!

Thus real expansion became possible from September 1996 when I became locally based and the official welcome to mark the beginning of the new era was held on Sunday 22 September 1996 at 2.30 pm with the Rev Dr Brian Powley (Chair of District) leading the service and the

Rev Kenneth Street (Methodist Property Office, Manchester) visiting to preach. With support of both the Connexion and the District it was not then difficult to persuade the Circuits also to join in, and pulpits were opened in the Circuits of the District as follows:

6 October 1996 Nantwich Circuit: 11.00am Woore, 6.30pm Barbridge.

13 October 1996 Stoke South Circuit: 10.30am Sandford Hill, 6.00pm Victoria Road.

20 October 1996 Congleton Circuit: 11.00am Brookhouse Green, 2.30pm Congleton Edge.

27 October 1996 Leek Circuit: 10.00am Endon, 2.30pm Meerbrook, 6.30pm Wetley Rocks.

3 November 1996 Hanley Circuit: 10.45am Milton, 6.00 pm Werrington.
(There were also two meetings that afternoon with the Vice President of Conference Ms. Jan Sutch Pickard 3.00pm Mow Cop and 3.45pm Englesea Brook)

10 November 1996 Biddulph and Mow Cop Circuit: 10.30 Brown Lees, 6.00 Hill Top, Biddulph Moor.

17 November 1996 Northwich Circuit: 10.45 Barnton, 6.30pm Weaverham.

24 November 1996 Sandbach and Alsager Circuit: 10.45 Rode Heath, 6.30 Hassall Road, Alsager.

1 December 1996 Newcastle Circuit: 9.00am St Peters, 10.30am St Peters.

8 December 1996 Burslem Circuit: 10.45am Longport, 6.00pm Hill Top.

15 December 1996 Kidsgrove Circuit: 11.00 Packmoor, 6.00pm Whitehill.

So it continued into 1997 with visits from 5 January to further circuits. For instance on the 5 January 1997 a visit was made to the Crewe Circuit for preaching as follows:10.30am Hightown, 2.30pm Weston and 6.00pm Wells Green.

If the Church and particularly the Methodist Church was one area that welcomed 'news coverage' from Englesea Brook the secular media was certainly another. The aim was to make a regular release of a new 'story' from Englesea Brook or offer a 'new angle' on an old story to feed local, regional and national newspapers, radio and television. There was always interest from the *Congleton Chronicle, the Crewe Chronicle, the Sentinel, the Methodist Recorder* and *BBC Radio Stoke*. Whether the story went any further then depended on a number of things: Just how 'new' and how 'different' was it? Was it really *new* news and not just re-cycled *old* news dressed up in new clothes! Was it interesting, and if so was it interesting to at least part of the secular population and not just religious folk? Was it surprising, unexpected, remarkable? If so it might hit the bull's eye - particularly if just the right eye-arresting headline could be found. Then it might reach national level!

This is how it worked:

Contact with BBC Radio Stoke led to fairly regular interviews often on Sunday morning but also sometimes during the week, especially with Barbara Adams. This flagged up Primitive Methodism and Englesea Brook within a wider BBC network as a place that was 'making news'. So when it was judged by the BBC 'lookouts' that there was a particularly good Primitive Methodist 'story' then regionally or nationally the 'big boys' also clocked in. Here are just a few of the opportunities that the media gave to keep Englesea Brook on the map:

BBC Radio Stoke interview conducted with George Groom, David Scott and Stephen Hatcher (4 April 1997).

Faith Lawrence, BBC Radio Manchester, New Broadcasting House, Oxford Road (Wed 21 Jan 2004).

Annabel Hampson, *Just a Moment*, ITV Gas Street, Birmingham (14 July 2004).

Terry Walsh, Radio Stoke Sun am (13 Aug 2004).

BBC Radio Stoke (22 Aug 2004).

BBC team of four from London with Ged Gray, Grace Darling Singers and Sally Drage (29 Jan 2005).

Dick Taylor, Crow TV, London (23 Feb 2005).

Ged Gray, BBC2 *The Battle for the Soul of Britain* Room 5007 BBC Manchester (9 Mar 2006).

Broadcasts also took place occasionally for the BBC nationally with people in the public eye such as Shaky (Shakin' Stevens) who had a Primitive Methodist ancestor, and Terry Jones (of Monty Python fame) who similarly had Primitive Methodist ancestry. A team represented Englesea Brook on the BBC programme *Eggheads*. The 'child funeral' programme also made it on to Russell Howard's *Good News* show as well as BBC Children's Newsround. However the staple diet was locally with Lamont Howie on Radio Stoke - and this served the cause very well.

There was another area of activity that brought an unexpected benefit. For instance the book sale brought customers seeking a wide range of books. The Rev Dr Robert Bates was undertaking research on the 'Resistance of the Confessing Church to Hitler' (6 Apr 2005) There was a vast turnover of books managed through Englesea Brook at that time and he asked: Could we look out for titles for him? The answer was that we could and did and found a range of material that included 20th Century German theology as context and also books with a clear focus - we found stories of former Primitive Methodists who in the 1940s opposed Hitler.

One was Jock Ellison Platt a Methodist Minister with Primitive Methodist background. He was imprisoned at Colditz for nearly the whole of WW2. Another was Arthur Baddeley, a local trade union leader and also a former Primitive Methodist. He was a leader of the campaign to re-build Lidice - a community that Hitler had razed to the ground as an act of vengeance. Schools were then given coverage of these themes in the 1940s / WW2 programme. There was further benefit in that Arthur Baddeley was also a local man and it was possible to track down his daughter who lived locally and hear the story from her lips also.

In both of these lives the theme of 'Resurrection' was vividly displayed. At the end of World War Two Colditz was liberated by Allied Forces. Jock Ellison Platt returned to circuit work in the UK and went on to tell his story. It can be found in: Duggan, Margaret, *Padre in Colditz,* London, H & S (1978). However with the cessation of hostilities Arthur Baddeley did not return to a life of ease: with Dr Barnett Stross he led the campaign to rebuild the town of the Lidice which Hitler had razed to the ground. At Lidice where once there were 'ashes' there are now homes and rose gardens thanks to Arthur Baddeley. The doors of many homes in Stoke-on-Trent were also opened and despite the abject poverty of those in Stoke-on-Trent at the termination of the war 'orphans' again became part of families.

The essence of Englesea Brook has been to continue to bring new ideas to birth. The aim was always to 'think big' in the range of programmes offered. Undoubtedly there have been 'purists' who criticised some of the school programmes that were undertaken in my time. The argument was that these programmes weren't mainly about Primitive Methodism in the 'form' that the critic recognised. What have the Romans who lived two thousand years ago to do with Primitive Methodism which only came to birth 200 years ago? What has the 1940s to do with Primitive Methodism - don't you know that Methodist Union took place in 1932 a decade earlier?

The answer is partly that the *Romans* programme provides a new way into the life and teaching of Christ. Further the answer is that this is just the kind of thing that 20thC Primitive Methodists would have endorsed. In the years immediately prior to WW1 and in the 1920s through their large, successful, polished and well-educated Sunday School movement the Primitive Methodists themselves were looking for new ways of exploring old stories. They would have warmed to the thought of using a Roman framework to tell the stories of Jesus - especially if the children could become Roman soldiers while the story was told.

As far as the 1940s are concerned I would like to assure you that not every Primitive Methodist dropped dead at midnight when the clock struck for Methodist Union. The lives of *former* Primitive Methodists in the 1940s had been steeped in their earlier experiences as Primitive Methodists.

Here is a choice between two churches today. One has Sunday services - full stop. The other has Sunday services plus a study group, Mothers and Toddlers, a Women's Fellowship and even a Youth Club. Can you really say that the former is superior and disallow the latter as a Church because of its varied activities and outreach?

Question: In personal life and in corporate church life, how can new ground be broken today?

Baptism proclaims God's offer of life in all its fullness at the beginning of life

The ceremonies of baptism, marriage and death were each given some focus at Englesea Brook as they were of course in the Primitive Methodist movement. Here was mission from the cradle to the grave.

Death was given a focus in the re-enacted role-play of the funeral of a working-class child. Baptism and Marriage were given a focus on two separate occasions with a display of costumes that filled the chapel and related to these themes; the wedding display being timed to correspond with the date of the marriage of Prince William and Kate Middleton.

The display shows some of the historic baptismal gowns that were hung at the front of the chapel, others were laid over pews upstairs and downstairs, and some were also hung in the museum room. It was amazing to discover just how many family heirlooms were offered for display. The oldest costume in bottle green was dated by the Chester Museum as originating in the 15th Century and this made the Primitive Methodist garments seem positively modern!

Working children

In the shadow of three crosses is the memorial stone to three working children.   The information about their life, work and early death has been taken from printed Primitive Methodist sources.   Just three of the victims of the capitalist system in the early years of the 19th Century were:

John Callen, Port Shipping, Coal Miner, died 1841, aged 10 years
Ann Buckley, Bolton, Errand Girl, died 1835, aged 10 years
Thomas Twigg, Hollington, Brickyard Worker, died 1823, aged 14 years

The three crosses also represent three real people who died a vicious death in the hands of the representatives of their society - that was two thousand years ago.
In a world where there is still vast injustice it is possible for visitors to find some strength for the future both in the memorial stone (these children were cogs in the capitalist society but are not forgotten!) and in the central empty cross (the eternal symbol of God's love).

It was tragedy then, and a tragedy today that in many parts of the world children are still working and dying in similar situations and at a similar age.

Painting of a cloud 360 degrees

This image by a young artist from a visiting school group speaks about the perspective of the viewer.   For most of life the perspective of the viewer is limited.   Yes it is possible to turn the head through 360 degrees and see something in every direction.   But there are people in the way or there is a bend in the road and a hill in the way. However at Mow Cop summit it is possible to see though 360 degrees with ease.

At Mow Cop summit pilgrims have even discovered that as they view through the points of the compass the 'finite' is transformed into the 'infinite'.   Visitors have journeyed to Mow Cop summit over hundreds of years; many have found 'God' as part of a 'life' that is now much bigger.   The question 'How far can you see?' receives the answer 'Very much further'.

In much of life *vision* is restricted: There are so often 'foreground objects' that conceal or a least obscure our vision.   At Mow Cop summit a full 360 degree view is possible.

Postscript

The point has been made in what has been written so far: From 1983 Englesea Brook Chapel and Museum was never intended to be either just a traditional chapel or a traditional museum. The vision that unfolded during the years 1983-2011 was focused in three ways:

1) The importance of the educational programmes and work with schools. This was an area of outreach that was unique within Methodism. Engagement with schools, as a visit to schools or as a visit from schools to Englesea Brook, was warmly welcomed by the schools themselves. When some specific programmes requested by schools were no longer available at Englesea Brook (post 2011) they took place for a few years at Mow Cop. Work with children was always a very high priority.

2) The importance of building in 'sustainability' and 'viability'. The nearer the project can grow to being self-sufficient the better. The Methodist Church at District and Connexional level has been most supportive, but this will not continue for ever. The Methodist Church itself nationally and locally has experienced major contraction now for many decades. If Englesea Brook wants a future then there is a goal to be reached - to develop to being as near to self-sufficiency as is humanly possible. Book-sales did a great deal to achieve this and it is wonderful that the Hassall Road Book Emporium maintains this tradition. Continue to work at it!

3) The importance of continuing with vision. The twin pillars of the success of Englesea Brook have been 'bright ideas' and 'hard work'. Continue to hold on to them both and the project will go from strength to strength for the glory of God and the benefit of our society. Here is an adaptation of a well- known saying of Saint Paul: 'Conviction, hard work and vision abide, and the greatest of these is *vision*'.

Action: What three ideas could you now take forward that you could prayerfully discuss with another, and that you might try out/apply in your own Church situation?